Acting Edition

Golden Shield

by Anchuli Felicia King

Copyright © 2023 by Anchuli Felicia King
All Rights Reserved

GOLDEN SHIELD is fully protected under the copyright laws of the United States of America, the British Commonwealth, including Canada, and all member countries of the Berne Convention for the Protection of Literary and Artistic Works, the Universal Copyright Convention, and/or the World Trade Organization conforming to the Agreement on Trade Related Aspects of Intellectual Property Rights. All rights, including professional and amateur stage productions, recitation, lecturing, public reading, motion picture, radio broadcasting, television, online/digital production, and the rights of translation into foreign languages are strictly reserved.

ISBN 978-0-573-71024-7

www.concordtheatricals.com
www.concordtheatricals.co.uk

FOR PRODUCTION INQUIRIES

UNITED STATES AND CANADA
info@concordtheatricals.com
1-866-979-0447

UNITED KINGDOM AND EUROPE
licensing@concordtheatricals.co.uk
020-7054-7298

Each title is subject to availability from Concord Theatricals Corp., depending upon country of performance. Please be aware that *GOLDEN SHIELD* may not be licensed by Concord Theatricals Corp. in your territory. Professional and amateur producers should contact the nearest Concord Theatricals Corp. office or licensing partner to verify availability.

CAUTION: Professional and amateur producers are hereby warned that *GOLDEN SHIELD* is subject to a licensing fee. The purchase, renting, lending or use of this book does not constitute a license to perform this title(s), which license must be obtained from Concord Theatricals Corp. prior to any performance. Performance of this title(s) without a license is a violation of federal law and may subject the producer and/or presenter of such performances to civil penalties. Both amateurs and professionals considering a production are strongly advised to apply to the appropriate agent before starting rehearsals, advertising, or booking a theatre. A licensing fee must be paid whether the title(s) is presented for charity or gain and whether or not admission is charged. Professional/Stock licensing fees are quoted upon application to Concord Theatricals Corp.

This work is published by Samuel French, an imprint of Concord Theatricals Corp.

No one shall make any changes in this title(s) for the purpose of production. No part of this book may be reproduced, stored in a retrieval system, scanned, uploaded, or transmitted in any form, by any means, now known or yet to be invented, including mechanical, electronic, digital, photocopying, recording, videotaping, or otherwise, without the prior written permission of the publisher. No one shall share this title(s), or any part of this title(s), through any social media or file hosting websites.

For all inquiries regarding motion picture, television, online/digital and other media rights, please contact Concord Theatricals Corp.

MUSIC AND THIRD-PARTY MATERIALS USE NOTE

Licensees are solely responsible for obtaining formal written permission from copyright owners to use copyrighted music and/or other copyrighted third-party materials (e.g. artworks, logos) in the performance of this play and are strongly cautioned to do so. If no such permission is obtained by the licensee, then the licensee must use only original music and materials that the licensee owns and controls. Licensees are solely responsible and liable for clearances of all third-party copyrighted materials, including without limitation music, and shall indemnify the copyright owners of the play(s) and their licensing agent, Concord Theatricals Corp., against any costs, expenses, losses and liabilities arising from the use of such copyrighted third-party materials by licensees. For music, please contact the appropriate music licensing authority in your territory for the rights to any incidental music.

IMPORTANT BILLING AND CREDIT REQUIREMENTS

If you have obtained performance rights to this title, please refer to your licensing agreement for important billing and credit requirements.

GOLDEN SHIELD was first produced by Melbourne Theatre Company at The Sumner, Southbank Theatre, Melbourne on 12 August with the following cast and creatives:

CAST

RICHARD WARREN/LARRY MURDOCH..........Nicholas Bell
EVA CHEN/DEPUTY MINISTER TAO
FUZHI..Jing-Xuan Chan
MEI HUANG/DEPUTY MINISTER GUO
SHENGWEI...................................... Gabrielle Chan
JULIE CHEN ....Fiona Choi
LI DAO.. Yi Jin
MARSHALL MCLAREN ....Josh McConville
AMANDA CARLSON/JANE BOLLMAN ....Sophie Ross
THE TRANSLATOR .... Yuchen Wang

CREATIVE

Director... Sarah Goodes
Dramaturg... Chris Mead
Set & Costume Design .... The Sisters Hayes (Esther Marie & Rebecca Hayes)
Lighting Designer .... Damien Cooper
Composter & Sound Designer..........................Luke Smiles
Voice & Dialect Coach........................Geraldine Cook-Dafner
Associate Designer.. Kat Chan
Assistant Director .... Alice Qin
Stage Manager ....Pippa Wright
Assistant Stage Manager .... Lisette Drew
Design Secondment..............................Jemima Johnston
Voice & Dialect Secondment .... Matt Furlani

CHARACTERS

RICHARD WARREN/LARRY MURDOCH
EVA CHEN/DEPUTY MINISTER TAO FUZHI
MEI HUANG/DEPUTY MINISTER GUO SHENGWEI
JULIE CHEN
LI DAO
MARSHALL MCLAREN
AMANDA CARLSON/JANE BOLLMAN
THE TRANSLATOR

SETTING

Washington D.C., Beijing, Yingcheng, Dallas, Sydney.

TIME

2006–2016

AUTHOR'S NOTES

Text Note

Bold text is spoken in Mandarin and synchronously translated into English by the Translator.

Bold and underlined text is spoken in Mandarin, and not necessarily accompanied by a translation.

Where noted, a 'staggered' translation occurs with a slight delay, as though being translated in real time.

Whenever the / symbol appears within the dialogue, it is to indicate an overlap of speech with the previous line of dialogue.

A Note About the Translator

The Translator is an intermediary between the audience and the action.

They intervene in the action only when their presence becomes essential.

They are otherwise engaged in an act of self-abnegation.

Playwright's Note

I read something on the internet.

This is how most of my plays start. It's also how the majority of the world's population gets its information. As of April 2019, 56.1% of the world's population was online. 55% of that content was written in English, and 800 million of those users were Chinese, making it by far the largest national population online.

And yes, I got those statistics from the internet.

It's easy to balk at statistics like these, but how can we actually conceptualize the human cost of this mass global digitalization? Indeed, how can we conceptualize the internet? As a nebulous cloud of data? As a vast, interconnected web of servers, data processing centers, household objects (the internet of things)? Or should we think of it as pure math – algorithms that determine what we see or don't see, algorithms written by an emergent class of technocrats who increasingly define our political, social and cultural lives?

To my mind, the theatre is really good place to grapple with impossibly big phenomena like the internet and globalization – what some contemporary philosophers, borrowing terminology from computer science, call 'metaobjects.' Theatre is uniquely suited to dealing with metaobjects because it's an aggressively immediate and analog form. It's a space where big issues can be transformed into little stories, where the epic and the quotidian don't just coexist but coalesce. In theater, the personal is always political, and vice versa.

In 2016, I read something on the internet. A group of Chinese dissidents were mounting a class action lawsuit against an American technology company for their purported criminal collusion with the Chinese government. The plaintiffs alleged that this billion-dollar corporation had knowingly helped the Chinese government build systems that would enable online censorship and digital surveillance as part of the Golden Shield project, the national security policy that has since become synonymous with China's Great Firewall.

For some ineffable reason, I knew I wanted to write a play about this. And I knew that the play should be written in both Mandarin and English, so the play would need a translator. And if it needed a translator, why not make them The Translator, who could not only translate literal text but also subtext and context, revealing the total sum of semiotic misfires that can happen when two parties try to bridge a communicative chasm?

I read everything I could find about the lawsuit. Then I read a lot more. I read public documentation on the numerous cases *Golden Shield* is based on. I read transcripts of civil trials, theses on the Great Firewall, books on digital filtering, on Mandarin-to-English translation, on the surveillance state and linguistics and technocracy... and then I threw it all out and tried to write a compelling piece of drama.

So how "real" are the events in this play? I would say the broader circumstances and events are based on fact, while individual characters and events are heavily fictionalized. In this sense, the play is itself an act of translation. Complex global issues are mapped onto fictive human stories – the core of which is the story of Julie and Eva, two Chinese-American sisters struggling to navigate their fraught relationship and shared trauma. The Chen sisters are in many ways my metaphor for the toxic sisterhood of China and America, two economically codependent superpowers that continue to struggle with their profound ideological incompatibility.

I am, of course, painfully aware of the hubris of a 25-year-old Thai-Australian playwright thinking she has anything meaningful to say about Sino-American relations (or indeed, about international litigation or human rights abuses in China). My hope is that *Golden Shield* gives you an impressionistic sweep of these metaobjects, and if you want to learn more about them, please consult an actual expert who will have far more interesting and nuanced things to say than I ever could. That is after all the wonderful thing about the internet – the enlightened texts of linguists, engineers, activists and lawyers are just a click away.

The only thing we're really qualified to do as artists is ask questions about what it means to be human. The heart of this play is a universal human predicament: the failure to communicate. *Golden Shield* explores how we fail to translate effectively on all fronts – not just between different languages and cultures, but between technologies, judicial systems, lovers and family members. I hope that what people take away from the play is that the *attempt* to translate, as fraught as it is, is what counts – that as multivalent and impossible as communication is, we have to keep trying because it's the best mechanism we have.

With a $4.6 million investment by MTC and MTC's Playwrights Giving Circle, the NEXT STAGE Writers' Program has introduced the most rigorous playwright commissioning and development process ever undertaken by the Company, setting a new benchmark for play development in Australia.

Golden Shield was the first NEXT STAGE original produced by the company.

Thank you to MTC's Playwrights Giving Circle for sharing our passion and commitment to Australian stories and Australian writers.

Louise Myer and Martyn Myer ao
Maureen Wheeler ao and Tony Wheeler ao
Christine Brown Bequest
Allan Myers ac qc and Maria Myers ac
Tony Burgess and Janine Burgess
Dr Andrew McAliece and Dr Richard Simmie
Larry Kamener and Petra Kamener

Thanks to Ian Potter Foundation, Naomi Milgrom Foundation, Myer Foundation, Malcolm Robertson Foundation, University of Melbourne.

ACT ONE

TRANSLATOR. The most difficult... the most difficult.
I guess it would be the proverbs.
I generally opt for a literal translation
'Stone' to 'stone'
And let the hearer extrapolate
Well, take something like 'every rose has its thorns'
That's pretty universal.
But for something culturally entrenched
Or by some degrees removed
That's a little trickier
An example:
三个和尚没水喝 (Sān gè héshàng méi shuǐ hē.)
Three monks have no water to drink.
Any thoughts?
(Laughing.) Right. Doesn't work so well.
So what do I do with that?
I can try to find an English equivalent, if one exists.
But of course, I risk making false parallels
Unwittingly engaging in an act of... linguistic imperialism
Or I can really spell it out –
Here's the monks, here's the water
Here's what that all means
But you do lose some of the beauty
Of the original
It'll be much the same with this job
I suspect
I tend to employ a kind of... hybrid approach
A bit of one-to-one, a bit of analogy,

Context where you need it
A word of warning though
Things can get... muddy
Once we really get going

I always tell my clients, 'give your mind time to adjust'.
It can be disorienting, hearing multiple voices at once
Just settle into it
Trust that your mind is a machine
Eventually, it'll find a focal point
Having said that,
It is essential that you concentrate

JULIE. *(Out.)* There's a lot of jargon in this case. A lot of legal jargon and a lot of technical / jargon.

MARSHALL. You've got IDS devices at the local router level, you've got provincial ISPs doing their own shit, so by the time you get to the / border AS –

JULIE. My advice to you is this: don't get caught up in the jargon. Jargon is one of many tactics employed by corporations like the defendant –

THE TRANSLATOR. ONYS Systems.

JULIE. – to evade accountability. Because they assume that the layman – and don't be offended, but that's you and me – simply can't understand what it is they do. What they build.

JANE. *(To MARSHALL.)* When I say call me back, you / have to –

MARSHALL. I'm busy, Bollman.

JANE. You have to / call me back.

JULIE. That's not what this case is about.

MARSHALL. I'm busy, someone's suing us?

JANE. Yes, I've been trying / to –

MARSHALL. Who's suing us?

JANE. Eight Chinese dissidents.

JULIE. This is about right and wrong.

MARSHALL. ...what?

JANE. Eight / Chinese –

MARSHALL. I heard you – fucking, what?

JULIE. You don't need to understand jargon to understand that.

EVA. What does that mean exactly, the Law of Nations?

MEI. <u>**What did you do?**</u>

那你是什么？/你干了什么？

Nà nǐ shì shénme?/Nǐ gànle shénme?

LI. <u>**I can't survive without you.**</u>

没有你我活不下去的。

Méiyǒu nǐ wǒ huóbuxiàqù de.

JANE. Eight Chinese dissidents are suing us for criminal collusion with the Chinese government.

MARSHALL. The – how? What? In China?

JANE. In... Texas.

MARSHALL. ...*how?*

JANE. It has to do with... pirates.

RICHARD. / It's about *pirates*.

JULIE. *(Out.)* Having said that, I have some legal jargon to get out of the way. The fact is that in this case the plaintiffs are not American citizens. They are eight citizens of the People's Republic of China. And they are suing the defendants –

THE TRANSLATOR. ONYS Systems.

JULIE. – for injuries inflicted in the state of China. So I imagine you're a little confused / I imagine you're wondering what the hell this has to do with you as a resident of Dallas County. And to explain that, I'm going to tell you about a piece of legislation called the Alien Tort Statute.

THE TRANSLATOR. D.C., 2012

RICHARD. It's about *pirates*.

JULIE. I'm aware of / the –

RICHARD. I mean I'd never even heard of this thing, you know why I'd never heard of it? Because it's from the Judiciary Act of 1789. Wherein this statute was included, I'm informed by the best and brightest legal historians, as a means for dealing with / pirates.

JULIE. Pirates.

RICHARD. Pirates. As in 'yarr'.

JULIE. Is that your *pirate*?

RICHARD. Maybe, why, what's your pirate?

JULIE. ...ahoy?

RICHARD. You're a disgrace to the legal profession.

JULIE. You said *yarr*.

RICHARD. Jules, I just don't wanna be that firm.

JULIE. I hear you.

RICHARD. I don't wanna just jump on some fad legal loophole just because every other schmuck on the human rights beat is doing it.

JULIE. It's not a fad.

RICHARD. I mean God knows your little humanitarian hobby is taking up enough billable hours –

JULIE. Well, I'm sorry doing my civic duty isn't proving to be a particularly profitable venture / for you.

RICHARD. That's not what I – don't put words in my mouth, Jules. I just mean that the last thing we can afford right now is some kinda academic exercise –

JULIE. It's / not –

RICHARD. – in whether or not a district judge will uphold an eighteenth-century statute. A statute which, I'll remind you, was not *intended* for a modern court of law but for marauding gangs of Vitamin-C-deficient *pirates*.

JULIE. It's not an academic exercise. Look, *Kpadeh v. Emmanuel*, tried in Florida last month, under the ATS.

THE TRANSLATOR. Alien Tort Statute.

JULIE. Twenty-two million in damages.

RICHARD. Jules, that case was about a Liberian dictator wiping his ass with the Geneva Convention. You wanna use this thing, you gotta have something that's flagrantly violating the Law of Nations.

JULIE. Okay. What about an oppressive government that casually engages in torture, censorship and ethnic genocide?

RICHARD. Well, which government are we talking about here? About seventeen are coming to mind. *(Beat.)*

Aw Jules! Not the China thing!

JULIE. I know it's not much to be going on.

RICHARD. No, no, I'm sorry, just because your comrade at / that Australian NGO –

JULIE. Amanda's not my *comrade*, okay, I / don't have *comrades*.

RICHARD. – has you all hot and bothered about some leaked document –

JULIE. It's an internal ONYS document that explicitly *shows* –

RICHARD. It's a bullet point!

JULIE. But –

RICHARD. A bullet point. You don't mount a case around a bullet point.

JULIE. It proves that they knowingly colluded with the CCP.

THE TRANSLATOR. Chinese Communist Party.

RICHARD. Jules, you've got a stick up your ass about the Chinese government lately, fine, go sign a petition. We don't go suing billion-dollar multinationals under obscure statutes just to make a point, we're not that *firm*.

JULIE. Rich, think of the precedent. If we could get some dissidents willing to sign on as plaintiffs, we get a class action going –

RICHARD. Woah, now we're talking about a class action?

JULIE. We'd have foreign citizens suing a multinational corporation. In a US district court. Doesn't that get you going just a little? Come on. It's the white whale of international humanitarian law.

RICHARD. Which district?

JULIE. I was thinking Dallas.

RICHARD. Dallas? Why Dallas?

JULIE. ONYS have an office in Fort Worth. Plus you passed the bar in Dallas.

RICHARD. You don't need me. Do it yourself, *pro hac vice*.

JULIE. Yeah, but then you wouldn't be my co-counsel.

RICHARD. You don't want me to co-counsel. *(Beat.)* Wait, you want me to co-counsel?

JULIE. It'd be a landmark case, Rich.

>   (*Beat.* **RICHARD** *is somewhat persuaded.*)

RICHARD. I don't have a problem with the humanitarian stuff, Jules. It's good for the firm. But if you're thinking about a class action here, that's a three, four-year timeline and a helluva lotta resources. It can't just be a gesture. It has to be… you know. Viable.

THE TRANSLATOR. Profitable.

JULIE. I hear you. Gimme a month. I'll dig around, see if it's viable.

RICHARD. Two weeks. And if you have to fly over there –

JULIE. Out / of my own pocket.

RICHARD. Out of your own pocket.

JULIE. Okay, but I want the paralegal.

RICHARD. No, no paralegal.

JULIE. Fuck you, why no paralegal?

RICHARD. I need him.

JULIE. What for?

RICHARD. The corporate liability shit, Jules. The shit that pays the bills.

>   (*Beat.*)

RICHARD. How's your Mandarin these days?

JULIE. Shot to shit. Why, you know any decent translators?

RICHARD. (*Knowingly.*) I mean.

JULIE. Rich. That's a terrible idea. (*Beat.*) Hey. That's not a terrible idea.

THE TRANSLATOR. D.C., 2012.

EVA. So it's like –

JULIE. You don't have to –

EVA. No, but I want to. So.

JULIE. Okay.

EVA. Okay, so it's like – a foreign citizen, or, I guess, citizens / plural?

JULIE. Right.

EVA. – can file in a US district court, but, only, or *specifically* if it's a lawsuit?

JULIE. Well, no, in torts.

EVA. Doesn't that –

JULIE. It's –

EVA. No, but a tort means a lawsuit, right?

JULIE. Torts is a whole branch of – Evie, you really don't have to *understand* the case.

EVA. But I –

JULIE. Because I'm not asking you / to –

EVA. And – 'in violation of the Law of Nations' –

JULIE. Evie.

EVA. What does that mean, exactly, the Law of Nations?

JULIE. Well, there's some debate about – that's why it's a sort of a loophole. I told you, right, it's kinda funny, it was actually, what it was *intended* for, was a way of dealing with –

EVA. Pirates. / Yeah.

JULIE. *Yarr.*

(Beat.)

EVA. It just doesn't seem like much to be going on.

JULIE. ...right.

EVA. And if the only evidence is this bullet / point –

JULIE. Actually, Evie, I didn't come for your legal opinion, okay, I'm a lawyer, I can form my own legal opinion, fuck.

> *(Beat.)*

EVA. Okay.

JULIE. So can you do it, or…

EVA. You are aware… this is D.C. Like, translators aren't few and far between.

JULIE. What, does it offend you, that I came to you with this?

EVA. I just like don't need a bailout.

JULIE. That's not what this is.

EVA. Like, I'm okay.

THE TRANSLATOR. 'I'm not okay.'

JULIE. It's not – it's not a bailout, okay? I gotta have someone I trust over there, we'll be dealing with some sensitive shit, some anti-CCP shit.

EVA. I just don't want you to think, like, because the last time we –

JULIE. No, I'm not – funerals are *weird*, dude. I'm not – I mean – water under the bridge.

THE TRANSLATOR. 'An idiom that generally refers to events that have happened in the past and are consequently no longer a source of concern. However, in this case, it means something like 'I'm still mad at you but let's not talk about it.'

JULIE. Just, you're being fucking weird, what is it, Evie? Did I offend you? I just… you kept up with the language and I didn't, so… that's all. That's all. I'm in a position, like I said, I have some new evidence and

Richard's supporting me in this, I mean he's not exactly *supporting* me, but you'd get a per diem and shit.

EVA. I don't know if I can. Timeline-wise.

JULIE. Timeline-wise, what does that mean, timeline-wise?

EVA. With my – you know I, like, applied to programs.

JULIE. Oh, uh.

EVA. What?

JULIE. I mean, it's – we've had this conversation.

EVA. What?

JULIE. It wasn't *programs,* you submitted a half-hearted application to Georgetown.

EVA. I might get in.

JULIE. *(Laughing.)* I admire your optimism.

THE TRANSLATOR. Roughly, 'you spent three years at Berkeley getting wasted, there's no way you're getting into Georgetown.'

(Beat.)

EVA. Yeah, so, I gotta go.

JULIE. Aw, what, you can't take a joke, come on, Evie.

EVA. That wasn't – you can't just –

JULIE. Lighten the fuck up, dude, DUDE, it was a joke.

EVA. You can't just, you can't just be a dick, and call it farce.

JULIE. Can't take a joke, Evie, shit.

EVA. This is a tired argument, so.

(Beat.)

JULIE. So what are you doing, then?

EVA. As in?

JULIE. As in, like, regular human survival shit. Do you have some kind of, I don't know, revenue stream?

EVA. I'm freelancing.

JULIE. Translating?

EVA. Translating isn't the only thing you can do with an Asia Studies major.

THE TRANSLATOR. 'I regret my choices and I'm essentially unemployable.'

JULIE. So what, you're temping? *(Beat.)* What are you, being fucking *coy*? What?

EVA. I don't wanna talk about it.

THE TRANSLATOR. 'I'm not talking about it.'

JULIE. The fuck, Evie, why not?

EVA. I just… I can't talk about it.

THE TRANSLATOR. 'I'm not talking about it, to *you*.'

JULIE. Because it's me?

EVA. Because a lot of things.

JULIE. Why?

EVA. As *I just said*. I *can't* –

THE TRANSLATOR. – 'won't' –

EVA. – *talk about it.*

JULIE. *(Joking.)* What is it, illegal? *(Beat.)* It's not illegal. Is it? Is it illegal?

EVA. I've said that I'm not talking about it, if that presents a problem to you, then, you know.

    (Beat.)

JULIE. Tell me it's not illegal.

EVA. It's not illegal.

JULIE. Are you lying to me?

EVA. No.

THE TRANSLATOR. 'Yes.'

JULIE. Okay.

EVA. It's not.

JULIE. Okay.

EVA. Strictly.

JULIE. *Evie.*

THE TRANSLATOR. There's some debate, as to whether or not Eva's profession is, in fact, legal.

JULIE. Are you –

EVA. This. Is Not. The Venue.

JULIE. Because –

EVA. For this. Discussion.

JULIE. Because I can't cover you under attorney-client privilege if / it's –

EVA. It's – I know this is somewhat impossible for you to *believe*, but I can take care of myself, I have been taking care of *myself*, you know, for *some* time now, I am a *person*, who *functions* independently, of you.

JULIE. But –

EVA. WILL YOU LIKE TRUST THAT I'M NOT BROKEN, FOR JUST ONCE IN YOUR FUCKING LIFE, CAN YOU TRUST THAT.

    (Beat.)

JULIE. I don't think you're broken.

EVA. Yeah, yeah, you do. But it's fine.

(Beat.)

JULIE. It's Beijing, Evie. It's just... being there, it'll be so...

EVA. I know.

JULIE. And so soon after mom.

EVA. I know.

JULIE. Just – don't write it off, okay? I... I would like to do this for you. Okay?

(Beat.)

EVA. What's it say?

JULIE. What?

EVA. The bullet point. What's it say?

THE TRANSLATOR. Dallas, 2015.

JULIE. Could you state your name and occupation for the record?

MARSHALL. Marshall McLaren. I'm the President of China Operations at ONYS Systems.

JULIE. Thank you. Mr. McLaren, could you tell us when you had your first consultancy with the Chinese Ministry of Public Security?

MARSHALL. In 2004.

JULIE. And then your contract was renewed in 2006?

MARSHALL. Yeah.

JULIE. And when did you go public?

MARSHALL. Our IPO, was, yeah, the year before that. 2005.

JULIE. You opened at a market value of, let's see here, $27 billion?

MARSHALL. Pretty cheap, actually. $45 a share.

JULIE. And these days, that number is closer to, what?

MARSHALL. Look, I'm not a 'market' guy, Ms. Chen, you know, I'm in management, but I got into this as an engineer. So.

(Beat.)

JULIE. Okay then. *(Beat.)* What were you consulting on in 2004?

MARSHALL. ISP Efficiency in Border and Internal AS-Topologies in Greater China.

JULIE. That's a lot of acronyms, Mr McLaren.

MARSHALL. Not for my line of business.

JULIE. Okay, let's start with ISP, what's that?

MARSHALL. Internet service providers.

JULIE. Okay, so ISP Efficiency: you were trying to make the internet faster?

MARSHALL. More efficient, sure.

JULIE. And did you?

MARSHALL. Did we increase network efficiency?

JULIE. Yes.

MARSHALL. I'm proud to say we did that. By around four hundred percent.

JULIE. Congratulations.

MARSHALL. Thanks.

JULIE. Could you be a little more specific about what you mean when you say 'efficiency'?

(Beat.)

MARSHALL. No.

(Beat.)

JULIE. Okay... what aspect, or aspects, of the internet, were you trying to make more efficient?

MARSHALL. That's the thing about networks, Ms Chen. It's all somewhat interconnected.

THE TRANSLATOR. Beijing, 2006.

MARSHALL. The thing with the fucking food, right –

LARRY. I am begging you not to get into this.

MARSHALL. No, because, if every fucking night, we have to sit down to a roundtable with eight ministers –

LARRY. It's a / cultural –

MARSHALL. – this is the twenty-first – what are we, the fucking yakuza, is what I'm saying – I need my fucking laptop, now they're giving us this shit –

LARRY. No one's giving us shit.

MARSHALL. They are, Larry, they're giving us shit, it's polite Chinese shit, but it's shit nonetheless, and what I'm saying is, is – if we could have a meeting, *one meeting*, in an *office*, in an office with *desks*, I don't need another, another fucking five pots of steamed *whatever* or a fucking egg that's been fermented for a hundred years in a silk basket at the foothills of Mountain Fing-fong-fang –

LARRY. They're actually, they're quite good, the century eggs.

THE TRANSLATOR. Century eggs are a Chinese delicacy.

MARSHALL. *Rotten eggs*, Larry.

THE TRANSLATOR. They are not literally fermented for a century.

MARSHALL. They are hundred-year-old *rotten eggs*.

LARRY. It's traditional.

MARSHALL. Traditions die, Larry. Traditions, they just, I'm not saying they aren't *nice*, and, and *quaint*, but traditions, sometimes they need to *die*, and this *food* thing – this is a thing that *needs to die*. The, look, the next generation, the millennial Chinese, you don't see them doing this shit, do ya, you don't see Samsung China having fucking *dumpling meetings*. Because the world, *this* one, that we *presently* occupy, is a world where meetings happen in *offices,* in *office buildings* with *wifi* and, and, I don't know, at the very goddamn least, my laptop, Larry, my goddamn laptop.

LARRY. This is the Ministry of Public Security here, okay, these are not tech-savvy people, these are old-guard communists here.

MARSHALL. And now this, what they are calling it, this exhibition?

LARRY. Oh, *now* you wanna work?

MARSHALL. Woah, hey, you're the one –

LARRY. No, that was – you just caught me off guard.

MARSHALL. I'm not *procrastinating* here, I'm *frustrated* –

LARRY. Sorry, no, you're – you're right.

MARSHALL. I'm always right, Larry. So this, uh, the *(Looking at a document.)* the Comprehensive Exhibition on Chinese Information System. System?

LARRY. I thought it was rude to / correct –

MARSHALL. They not got plurals in Mandarin?

THE TRANSLATOR. They don't.

MARSHALL. Okay, so, what kinda demonstration are we talking about here?

LARRY. I, uh – the description is a bit... vague.

MARSHALL. *(Reading.)* 'Make efficient and consciously implement system for targeting obscene and harmful materials.' Lovely euphemism for porn.

LARRY. I think it's a bit of a mistranslation.

THE TRANSLATOR. It's not.

MARSHALL. 'Make efficient.'

THE TRANSLATOR. In Mandarin, the goal of the action is often inbuilt in the verb.

MARSHALL. Jesus.

THE TRANSLATOR. Actually, it's been suggested by linguists that this reflects two completely different patterns of thought. The Mandarin speaker thinks circularly, in a loop, while the English speaker thinks linearly, in a line. *(Beat.)* That's not strictly / relevant.

MARSHALL. Larry, what happens when the world's biggest flow of data – the packets of 1.3 billion users – goes through a single filtering system?

LARRY. Uh, it's – bad?

MARSHALL. Through one chokehold to the world wide web, Larry, what happens?

LARRY. Things get stuck.

MARSHALL. Things that aren't *supposed* to get stuck, get stuck. And things that aren't supposed to get *through,* get through. What else?

LARRY. It's slow?

MARSHALL. That's right, Larry. It's slow as shit. Because trying to sift through the online traffic of the world's largest fucking population is a pretty fucking *inefficient* process, it is in fact a *necessarily* inefficient – *(A realization.)* Larry.

LARRY. You're having / a –

MARSHALL. Yeah, I am, I am, Larry, Larry, what if it wasn't a single filtering system?

LARRY. ...you lost me.

MARSHALL. Why did I hire you?

LARRY. I'm the only guy who'll put up with you.

MARSHALL. I'm ignoring that. Larry, what if we decentralized the firewall?

LARRY. So – wait –

MARSHALL. The chokehold is at the border AS, right? But what if the filtering wasn't just happening at the national level?

LARRY. Uh.

MARSHALL. Think about it: three-tier structure, right? Local, provincial, national. You've got IDS devices at the local router level, you've got provincial ISP's doing their own shit, so by the time you get to the border AS –

LARRY. Wait, / Marsh.

MARSHALL. – the packet's already been through, what, twelve, thirteen different checkpoints. More IP blocking, more DNS hijacking, *and* you unclog the whole fucking system. And yes, I will accept my Nobel prize now.

LARRY. I don't know, Marsh.

MARSHALL. Why, cuz their hardware won't cut it? Yeah, that crossed my mind, but here's the fucking kicker, Larry: *we* build the routers. Not just the routers – I'm talking the whole architecture. Data centers, switches, access points. We don't just sell them an idea, Larry. We can sell them the fucking gear to do it.

(Beat.)

LARRY. Marsh, I mean – that's kind of a different ballgame.

MARSHALL. ...we're in IT, Larry. Don't do sport metaphors.

LARRY. You're talking about giving them a lot more, uh –

MARSHALL. A lot more... what?

LARRY. You know. 'Mileage.'

MARSHALL. *(Not getting it.)* Yeah. It's a faster topology. That's the point.

LARRY. That's not –

MARSHALL. That's the point, Larry.

LARRY. But you're not just talking about, like, filtering out content from the rest of the world, that's – you're talking about internal monitoring. At every level.

MARSHALL. Yeah, I mean, that's the way they're headed. They're just doing it inefficiently. We can make it efficient.

(Beat.)

LARRY. Anyway, you're talking about a huge overhaul, building them new infrastructure, I mean, jeez, we're supposed to be consulting / on –

MARSHALL. Larry, need I remind you here, we're building up to the fucking *Olympics* here –

LARRY. What / I'm –

MARSHALL. – you wanna talk about ballgames, that's the ballgame, Larry, the fucking Beijing Olympics, you heard about that little eight-figure ballgame?

LARRY. All we're contractually obligated to –

MARSHALL. It's called the *Golden Shield Project*.

THE TRANSLATOR. '金盾工程 jīndùn gōngchéng'

LARRY. They're just talking about blocking porn, for chrissakes, you don't need a total overhaul –

MARSHALL. But it's not called the no-porn project, is it, Larry? It's called the *Golden Shield* Project. That's a pretty fucking superlative name for a no-porn project, wouldn't you say, Larry? Almost like they're aiming at something a little more *grandiose*. And when you see the pharaoh drawing up the plans for the fucking pyramids, it's probably a good time to get into the brick business.

LARRY. Marsh, all I'm saying is, maybe we just give the client what they're actually asking for? Like, I'm just saying, you know, if all they're talking about right now, if all they're *willing* to talk to *us* about, is filtering out some porn, maybe we just deliver some basic ways of, like, filtering out some porn, is all I'm saying.

(Beat.)

MARSHALL. You know what I dream of, Larry?

LARRY. Marsh –

MARSHALL. No, no, let me finish, it's a really – it's a breathtaking dream, Larry, you're gonna want to hear this dream, Larry. I dream of a man. I dream of a meeting with a man.

LARRY. There are websites for that.

MARSHALL. Let me finish. This man is from State. No, better yet, Defense. And this man comes up to me, and he says to me, in simple, glorious, American English, 'Mr. McLaren, we'd like you to build the most efficient national network topology the world has ever seen. And if you choose to take on this *monumental* task, says the man from Defense, in addition to our eternal gratitude, we're gonna give you a ton of space, we're gonna give you a round-the-clock team of guys, we're gonna dedicate maximal resources to this endeavor because it is at the very top of our list, it is our number one national security priority.' And you know where this meeting happens, Larry?

LARRY. No.

MARSHALL. Me neither, but it sure as shit ain't a fucking dumpling house.

THE TRANSLATOR. Dallas, 2015.

JULIE. Mr McLaren, back in 2006, were you aware of the existence of an online forum known as Zhuangzi?

MARSHALL. You'd have to be pretty fu – you'd have to be pretty clueless to work in China, in my line of business, and not know about Zhuangzi. I'm not clueless.

JULIE. Could you answer / the –

MARSHALL. Yeah, I knew about Zhuangzi.

JULIE. What did you know about it?

MARSHALL. I knew it was an underground, sorta, online community, forum, people voicing their dissatisfaction about the government. Frequented by dissidents. *(Beat.)* Not that – I don't have a stance on – I'm just using the terminology.

JULIE. Of course.

MARSHALL. That's just, that's a fact, they're, they're deemed by, to be dissidents.

JULIE. Of course. *(Beat.)* Your contract with the Ministry was renewed in 2006?

MARSHALL. As I've said.

JULIE. Why did your geographical total increase?

MARSHALL. Sorry?

JULIE. In 2005, you reported that China made up 11% of your gross revenue. In 2006, that number jumps to a whopping 34%. Why'd you make more money in 2006?

(Beat.)

MARSHALL. I guess they liked us.

THE TRANSLATOR. Beijing, 2006.

MARSHALL. The fucking *weasels*.

LARRY. Marsh.

MARSHALL. *Now* they want a fucking *office meeting*, the fucking *weasels*.

LARRY. I know it looks bad.

MARSHALL. Wine and dine us for fifteen fucking months, then the day after we submit our fucking proposal suddenly it's fucking crumbling office brutalism in the fucking outskirts.

LARRY. It could be circumstantial, I mean, uh, I dunno, maybe they ran outta the food budget.

MARSHALL. You ever been dumped, Larry?

LARRY. I don't, uh –

MARSHALL. I've been dumped. I've been dumped a couple of times. That surprise you?

LARRY. Uh.

MARSHALL. Every time I got dumped, Larry, you know where the bitch took me? To a neutral zone. That's what's happening here, Larry. This is a Dear John letter. This is a 'it's not you, it's me and my latent daddy trauma.'

LARRY. I'm just saying, let's not get ahead of ourselves, it could be unrelated.

MARSHALL. Oh, get your head of your fucking ass, Larry, I'll tell you exactly what is going on here, we delivered a fucking weak-ass fucking parse-list filter for motherfucking *porn* – on your fucking *instruction* I might add – and now, okay, we're getting dumped, we're gonna lose the consultancy to some goddamn Chinese *monkeys* who can adequately copy my fucking IP.

LARRY. There was no guarantee –

MARSHALL. It's our fucking IP, Larry. It's *ours*.

LARRY. That's interesting.

MARSHALL. What is?

LARRY. Well, a second ago, you're all 'my IP' this, 'my IP' that, now you're saying 'our IP', it's just interesting. It's an interesting thing I observed.

MARSHALL. What is this, Larry? Is this an attempt at, at *passive aggression*? Is my *outsized ego* hampering your – you can get fucked, Larry. You told me to *withhold* my revolutionary fucking schematic, and *you're* the one getting butthurt? You can get fucked, Larry. You can get brutally sodomized. You can get ass-fucked with a rusted fucking –

(*Enter* **DEPUTY MINISTER GAO**.)

LARRY. Minister Gao, so good to see you! And…

(*He notices the* **TRANSLATOR**.)

THE TRANSLATOR. Don't mind me, I'm just the translator.

LARRY. Right. (*To the* **MINISTERS**.) Thank you for the wonderful dinner. I'm still full.

THE TRANSLATOR. **He thanks you for dinner and jokes that he is still full.**

他感谢您的晚餐,还开玩笑地说他现在还饱着呢。

Tā gǎnxiè nín de wǎncān, hái kāiwánxiàode shuō tā xiànzài hái baozhe ne.

DEPUTY MINISTER GAO. <u>Tell him the restaurant we will eat at next time is even better.</u>

告诉他，我们下次去一个更好的餐厅。

Gào sù tā, wǒ mén xià cì qù gèng hǎo de cān tīng.

THE TRANSLATOR. The Minister says the restaurant you will eat at next time is even better.

DEPUTY MINISTER GAO. <u>Better century eggs!</u>

那家的松花蛋更好吃。

Nǎ jiāde sōnghuādàn gènghao chī.

THE TRANSLATOR. More culinary delights. *(To the audience.)* What the Minister actually said was 'better century eggs' but given Marshall's aversion to them, I thought this was more appropriate.

MARSHALL. *(To* **LARRY.***)* See if you can get anything out of this / fuckin' weasel.

THE TRANSLATOR. *(To the* **MINISTER.***)* <u>He is saying 'see if you – '</u>

他在说：看你能不能 –

Tā zài shuō: kàn nǐ néngbùnéng.

MARSHALL. Uh – don't translate that.

LARRY. Marsh. Come on.

THE TRANSLATOR. *(To the audience.)* This is a good moment to mention that there are two kinds of translators.

MARSHALL. What, like she knows the word 'weasel'.

THE TRANSLATOR. Those who believe in normative ethics.

MARSHALL. Go on, ask her.

THE TRANSLATOR. – and those who don't.

MARSHALL. Ask her if she knows the word 'weasel'.

DEPUTY MINISTER GAO. <u>Is there a problem?</u>

出问题了吗?

Chūwèntí le ma?

THE TRANSLATOR. *(To the audience.)* I, for one, am something of a… chaotic neutral. That is why I'm about to inform the Minister that these men are conspiring to extract information from her. *(To* **GAO**.*)* <u>They're discussing their strategy for this meeting.</u>

他们正在讨论这个会议的策略。

Tāmen zhèngzài tǎolùn zhège huìyì de cèlüè

DEPUTY MINISTER GAO. <u>What are they saying?</u>

讨论什么?

Tǎolùn shénme?

THE TRANSLATOR. <u>They intend to ask you about something.</u>

他们准备问您一个事。

Tāmen zhǔnbèi wèn nín yígè shì.

DEPUTY MINISTER GAO. <u>About what?</u>

什么事?

Shénme shi?

THE TRANSLATOR. <u>They didn't say.</u>

他们没说。

Tāmen méi shuō.

LARRY. Is there a problem?

THE TRANSLATOR. Not at all. The Minister invites you to take a seat. *(To the* **MINISTER**.*)* <u>They're asking you to take a seat.</u>

他们请你就坐。

Tāmen qing ni jiùzuò.

LARRY. Thank you, *xie xie*.

MARSHALL. We tread carefully.

DEPUTY MINISTER GAO. *(Talking to the* **TRANSLATOR**.*)* <u>We should tread carefully.</u>

我们应该谨慎行事。

Wǒmen yīnggāi jǐnshen xíngshì.

THE TRANSLATOR. *(To the Audience.)* We're currently witnessing something I call 'philological parallelism'.

MARSHALL. Don't show our hand.

DEPUTY MINISTER GAO. *(To the* **TRANSLATOR**.*)* <u>Don't disclose anything.</u>

不要透露任何东西。

Búyào tòulù rènhé dōngxī.

THE TRANSLATOR. *(To the Audience.)* They're saying the same thing.

MARSHALL. *(To the* **TRANSLATOR**.*)* We're ready.

THE TRANSLATOR. *(To the Audience.)* They're ready. *(To the* **MINISTERS**.*)* <u>They're ready.</u>

他们准备好了。

Tāmen zhǔnbèi haole.

DEPUTY MINISTER GAO. <u>Tell him we're ready.</u>

告诉他我们准备好了。。

Gàosu tā wǒmen zhǔnbèi haole.

THE TRANSLATOR. *(To the guys.)* She's ready. *(To the Audience.)* We're ready.

DEPUTY MINISTER GAO. <u>First, / we would like to say we are very impressed with your work.</u>

首先，/我们想要说，我们对你的工作印象十分深刻。

Shǒuxiān,/wǒmen xiǎng yào shuō, wǒmen duì nǐ de gōngzuò yìnxiàng shífēn shēnkè.

THE TRANSLATOR. *(Staggered.)* First, we would like to say we are very impressed with your work so far.

DEPUTY MINISTER GAO. <u>The Ministry / feels that the Comprehensive Exhibition on Targeting Harmful and Obscene Materials in Chinese Information System was a great success.</u>

我部/认为，针对中国信息系统里有害淫秽内容的综合展览很

成功。

Wǒ bú rènwéi zhēnduì Zhōngguó xìnxīxìtǒnglǐ yǒuhài yínhuì nèiróng de zōnghé zhǎnlǎn hěn chénggōng.

THE TRANSLATOR. *(Staggered.)* The ministry feels that the Comprehensive Exhibition on Targeting Harmful and Obscene Materials in Chinese Information System was a great success.

DEPUTY MINISTER GAO. <u>Our purpose for calling this meeting / today is to start a dialogue about the possibility of contract extension between the Ministry of Public Security and ONYS Systems.</u>

我们今天开会的目的/是讨论公安部和ONYS系统是否能延续 合同。

Wǒmen jīntiān kāihuì de mùdì shì tǎolùn Gōngānbù hé ONYS xìtǒng shìfǒu néng yánxù hétong

THE TRANSLATOR. *(Staggered.)* Our purpose for calling this meeting today is to discuss the possibility of contract extension between the Ministry of Public Security and ONYS Systems.

MARSHALL. *(To* **LARRY.***)* That's it. That's the Dear John.

THE TRANSLATOR. <u>He / said –</u>

他/说 –

Tā shuō.

MARSHALL. Don't translate that. It's the Dear John, Larry.

LARRY. It doesn't sound like a Dear John, it sounds like an offer on the table.

MARSHALL. We wouldn't be *here* if there was a genuine offer, Larry, we'd be eating fucking dim sum, signing the dotted line. They've sent a mid-level bureaucrat to keep us haggling over the fine print for a couple of months, so they can get us to do some unpaid labor training their guys to implement our fucking schematics, and then they're gonna dump us.

LARRY. That is completely paranoid.

MARSHALL. No, no. We tried it your way. The only thing these people understand is a good deal. Time to sell them something. *(To the MINISTER.)* Respectfully, uh, Minister, we weren't entirely happy with the outcome of the Exhibition.

LARRY. *(Warning.)* Marsh.

MARSHALL. *(To the TRANSLATOR.)* Translate that.

THE TRANSLATOR. <u>They're saying they weren't happy with the outcome of the Exhibition.</u>

他们在说他们对展览取得的收入不是很满意。

Tāmen zài shuō tāmen duì zhǎnlǎn qǔdéde shōurù búshi hěn mǎnyì.

LARRY. What are you doing?

MARSHALL. *(To the MINISTER.)* We feel the limited scope of this consultation, has limited us in terms of, uh, our ability to address some of the more global issues with your system.

THE TRANSLATOR. *(Staggered.)* **They feel that the limited scope of this consultation has limited their work, they want to address bigger issues with your system.**

他们认为这次咨询的范围限制了他们的工作。他们想指出你 们系统里更主要的问题。

Tāmen rènwéi zhècì zīxún de fànwéi xiànzhì le tāmende gōngzuò. Tāmen xiang zhǐchū nǐmen xìtǒnglǐ gèng zhǔyào de wèntí.

DEPUTY MINISTER GAO. *(Smiling.)* **The insolence.**

傲慢。

Àomàn.

THE TRANSLATOR. *(Out.)* She thinks he's insolent.

DEPUTY MINISTER GAO. **What sort of issues?**

什么样的问题?

Shénmeyàng de wèntí?

THE TRANSLATOR. What sort of issues?

MARSHALL. We believe that efficiency is a much larger issue than we were able to fully address with our parse-list system for, uh, 'harmful and obscene materials', and, again respectfully, we think – if we were to become involved in Golden Shield, more thoroughly, in the lead-up to the Olympics – we could outline a new network topology, that would be much more efficient.

THE TRANSLATOR. *(Staggered.)* **He believes efficiency is a much larger issue. If their contract were to be renewed during the Olympics, they could design a system that would be much more efficient.**

他认为效率是最大的问题。如果合同在奥运会期间续签，他们应该能设计一个更有效率的系统。

Tā rènwéi xiàolǜ shì zuì dàde wèntí rúguǒ hétong zài Àoyùnhuì qījiān xùqiān, tāmen yīnggāi néng shèjì yígè gèngyǒuxiàolǜ de xìtǒng.

DEPUTY MINISTER GAO. *(Smiling, muttered to the* **TRANSLATOR.***)* <u>This is the first time I'm hearing any of this.</u>

他们从来没有说过。

Tamen conglai meiyou shuoguo.

THE TRANSLATOR. *(Out.)* This is the first time she's hearing any of this.

DEPUTY MINISTER GAO. <u>Perhaps there is some confusion about the goals of our project. The Ministry wants to increase efficiency through the refinement and modernization of our existing system. We value your expertise but we are not soliciting an American version of the Chinese internet.</u>

或许我们项目的目标有些模糊，但是我们想完善我们现有的 系统，使其现代化，从而提高效率。虽然你们的专业知识值 得肯定，但是我们并不需要一个美国版本的中国网络。

Huòxǔ wǒmen xiàngmù de mùbiāo yǒuxiē mohu, dànshì women xiǎng wánshàn wǒmen xiànyǒude xìtǒng. Shǐ qí xiàndàihuà cóngér tígāo xiàolǜ. Suīrán nǐmende zhuānyèzhīshi zhidekending, dànshì wǒmen bìng bù xuyao yígè Měiguó bǎnběn de Zhōngguó wǎngluò.

THE TRANSLATOR. *(Staggered.)* Perhaps there is some confusion on the part of your company about the goals of the Scientific Development policy. The Ministry seeks to increase efficiency through the refinement and modernization of our existing system. We value your expertise but we are not soliciting an American version of the Chinese internet.

MARSHALL. Respectfully, Minister, that's the thing, I'm having some difficulty working under the auspices of a development policy I've been given next to no information about.

THE TRANSLATOR. *(Staggered.)* **We are working under a policy we have been given no information about.**

关于我们遵守的政策，我们什么都不知道。

Guānyú wǒmen zūnshǒu de zhèngcè, women shenme dou buzhidao.

LARRY. *(Hissed.)* Marsh.

MARSHALL. If there was some transparency around your goals for this project, for Golden Shield, other than, you know, to 'make efficient', then maybe we could provide some actionable solutions.

THE TRANSLATOR. *(Out.)* This isn't going well. I'll just say he wants to know the goals. *(Beat.)* **He'd like some clarification on the goals for the project.**

他希望知道项目的明确目标。

Tā xīwàng zhīdào xiàngmù de míngquè mùbiāo.

(Beat.)

DEPUTY MINISTER GAO. *(To the* **TRANSLATOR.***)* **Put up the slide.**

打开幻灯片。

Dǎkāi huàndēngpiàn.

THE TRANSLATOR (LARRY, MARSHALL). She's asked me to put up the slide.

DEPUTY MINISTER GOU. **The primary goals / of the Golden Shield Project are as follows:**

金顿工程的主要目标如下

jīn dùn gōng chéng de zhǔ yào mù biāo rú xià

THE TRANSLATOR. The primary goals of the Golden Shield Project are as follows:

DEPUTY MINISTER GAO. <u>To increase China's digital security.</u>

加强中国的数据安全。

Jiāqiáng Zhōngguó de shùjù ānquán.

THE TRANSLATOR. *(Staggered.)* To increase China's digital security.

DEPUTY MINISTER GAO. <u>To target superstitious, pornographic, violent and other harmful information.</u>

针对迷信，淫秽，暴力还有其它的有害信息。

Zhēnduì míxìn, yínhuì, bàolì háiyǒu qítāde yǒuhài xìnxī.

THE TRANSLATOR. *(Staggered.)* To target superstitious, pornographic, violent and other harmful information.

DEPUTY MINISTER GAO. <u>And to combat internet crime by terrorist organizations like Zhuangzi and other hostile actors.</u>

另外还要严打由恐怖组织比如说庄子和其他反华分子造成的 网络犯罪。

lìng wài há yào yán dǎ yóu kǒng bù zǔ zhī bǐ rú shuō Zhuāngzǐ hé qí tā fǎn húa fèn zǐ zào chéng de wǎng luò fàn zuì

THE TRANSLATOR. *(Staggered.)* And to combat internet crime by terrorist organizations like Zhuangzi and other hostile actors.

DEPUTY MINISTER GAO. <u>We can make this document available to their Board.</u>

我们可以给他们董事会提供这个文件。

Wǒmen kěyǐ gěi tāmen dǒngshìhuì tígōng zhège wénjiàn.

THE TRANSLATOR. She says they are happy to make this document available to your board before you continue with these meetings.

LARRY. Thank you, for all of this, we will – we will definitely pass this document on.

THE TRANSLATOR. <u>She says he would like a copy.</u>

他说他想要一份拷贝文件。

Tā shuō tā xiǎngyào yífèn kǎobèi wénjiàn.

LARRY. *(To* **MARSHALL.***)* You happy? They're sharing their Orwellian goals.

MARSHALL. She's stalling. *(To the* **TRANSLATOR.***)* Don't translate that.

THE TRANSLATOR. Of course. *(To the* **MINISTERS.***)* <u>They think you're stalling.</u> *(To the Audience.)* I translated it.

I translated it.

他们认为你正在拖延时间。

Tāmen rènwéi nǐ zhèngzài tuōyán shíjiān.

MARSHALL. Look. Minister. I'm gonna level with you.

LARRY. *(Noise.)*

MARSHALL. You want a heavy-duty firewall. That's a fact. Right now, it's real slow. That's the second fact. Now here's the third fact: during the Olympics, it's gonna get a helluvalot slower. And what I'm saying is, eventually you're gonna have to confront the fact that the problem with the system – is the system itself. So to solve that problem, you have to change the system.

THE TRANSLATOR. *(Staggered.)* <u>You want a heavy-duty firewall. That's a fact. At the moment, it's slow. That's the second fact. Third fact: during the Olympics, it's</u>

going to get slower. You have to understand that the problem with your system is the system itself. To solve that problem, you have to change the system.

首先，你们想要个强大而坚固的防火墙。其次，现在系统比 较慢。最后，在奥运会期间，系统会更加慢。你们要认清 产生系统的问题是系统的本身。你们要解决这个问题的话，必须改换系统。

Shǒuxiān, nǐmen xiǎngyào gè qiángdà ér jiāngù de fánghuǒqiáng. Qícì xiànzài xìtǒng bǐjiào màn. Zuìhòu zài Àoyùnhuì qījiān, xìtǒng huì gèngjiāmàn。 Nǐmen yào rènqīng chǎnshēng xìtǒng de wèntí shì xìtǒng běnshēn。 Nǐmen yào jiějué zhège wèntí de huà, bìxū gǎihuàn xìtǒng.

DEPUTY MINISTER GAO. *(Rising.)* **We do not believe our internet needs to be changed. Thank you for offering your professional opinion and for this productive discussion.**

改换系统这个想法，我们并不赞成。谢谢您提供专业的建 议，并且参加这次高效的讨论。

Gǎihuàn xìtǒng zhège xiǎngfǎ, wǒmen bìng bú zànchéng. Xièxie nín tígōng zhuānyè de jiànyìo。 Bìngqiě cānjiā zheci gaoxiao de taolun.

THE TRANSLATOR. *(Staggered.)* We do not believe our internet needs to be changed. But thank you for offering your professional opinion and for this productive discussion.

MARSHALL. Wait, okay, tell her – that was the wrong – we're not proposing to *change* the system, okay, would you translate that? I'm not trying to *change* anything.

THE TRANSLATOR. *(Staggered.)* **He says he's not trying to *change* anything.**

他说他什么东西都不换。

Tā shuō tā shénme dōngxi dōu/dū bù huàn.

DEPUTY MINISTER GAO. <u>He is saying that our system has to be rebuilt?</u>

Tāde yìsi shì shuō wǒmen de xìtǒng xūyào chóngjiàn ma?

THE TRANSLATOR. *(Staggered.)* You are saying that our system has to be rebuilt?

MARSHALL. Not rebuilt, uh – iterated. Developed.

THE TRANSLATOR. *(Staggered.)* **Not rebuilt. Developed.**

不是重建，是改善。

Búshì chóngjiàn, shì gǎishàn.

MARSHALL. It is my professional opinion – having reviewed the latencies in your national AS topology –

THE TRANSLATOR. <u>It is my professional opinion – having reviewed the latencies in your system –</u>

我给的专业建议是针对你们系统延迟的问题 ...

Wǒ geide zhuānyè jiànyì shì zhendui nǐmen xìtǒng yánchíde dewenti.

LARRY. Marsh.

MARSHALL. – that what we can help you to do – that what it is you frankly *need* to do – is to decentralize your firewall.

(Beat.)

TRANSLATOR. A note about the word 'decentralize.'

There are two ways I can translate 'decentralize' into Mandarin. The first, 分散 (fen san.), means something like disperse, scatter. The second, closer to decentralize, is 下放 (xia fang.) Unfortunately, like many Mandarin verbs, it has multiple meanings: to let go, put aside, do away with.

Now, another translator, in an attempt to preserve Marshall's phraseology, might here tell the Minister that Marshall intends to disperse, or worse do away with, the national firewall. This would derail the meeting.

Happily, I am not that translator.

You see, I don't just understand the literalities of Marshall's proposal. I see the whole loop. Marshall McLaren is proposing an ingenious three-tiered firewall, one that will exponentially increase the government's ability to filter and inspect the online activities of their citizenry. It will come to be called the Great Firewall, and finding ways to climb it will become a national pastime.

In other words, Marshall is talking about an increase in control, an increase in efficiency, effected *through* decentralization but not resulting *in* it. So all I have to do is change one little word. I turn to the Minister, and I say:

(To the **MINISTER.***)* **He wants to centralize the firewall.**

他想构建一个更集中的防火墙。He wants to centralize the firewall.

DEPUTY MINISTER GAO. <u>More centralized?</u>

更集中.

THE TRANSLATOR. *(Back to the* **MINISTER.***)* <u>That's what he said.</u>

他是这样说的。

Tā shì zhèyàng shuōde.

Because in this case, paradoxically, centralize is the more efficient translation.

DEPUTY MINISTER GAO. <u>We... could consider that.</u>

这一点 ... 我们可以考虑。

Zhè yì diǎn… wǒmen kěyǐ kǎolǜ.

THE TRANSLATOR. The Ministry would be interested in reviewing such a proposal.

LARRY. Uh. They would?

MARSHALL. They would?

THE TRANSLATOR. Dallas, 2015.

JULIE. Now to be honest, we don't have an extensive paper trail of ONYS' dealings with the Ministry, for the simple reason that these dealings were mostly conducted in China.

But a document we *do* have access to, our exhibit A, is a leaked ONYS document. And specifically, I'm going to direct your attention to the third bullet point that features in that document, a bullet point that reads as follows: 'to combat internet crime by terrorist organizations like Zhuangzi and other hostile actors.'

THE TRANSLATOR. Beijing, 2012.

EVA. Can I, uh, if ask you a question, can you be like, really honest?

JULIE. That's sort of my default.

EVA. Is this like… are you actually trying to win this case? Or is it, like, a symbolic gesture?

JULIE. Um, fuck you.

EVA. Hey, that's like an honest question, it's not loaded.

JULIE. The two aren't mutually exclusive, you know.

EVA. Because, like, I'm no expert –

JULIE. You're really not.

THE TRANSLATOR. You can probably guess, but, uh, roughly, 'you're stupid'.

(Beat.)

EVA. Forget it.

JULIE. Hey, no, Evie –

EVA. No, no, I can be your ventriloquist dummy for a week, it's what I signed up for, so.

JULIE. No, fuck, it's my bad, dude. My brand of humor is – I can be a little –

EVA. Mercenary?

JULIE. I was gonna say... zesty.

(Beat.)

Hey, it's really different, right?

EVA. What?

JULIE. This area. It's like... Singapore or something.

EVA. Oh. Yeah. Gentrified.

JULIE. Definitely.

EVA. And like, all this nightlife? I don't remember, like, bars.

JULIE. In full fairness, we were –

EVA. Yeah, no, sure, that's not the sort of thing you notice, as a kid.

JULIE. And I suspect the absence of someone screaming her head off at us –

EVA. Yeah, that probably contributes to the different... atmosphere.

(Beat.)

THE TRANSLATOR. I feel this is the point to interject with some context. Julie and Eva spent their childhood primarily in suburban D.C. but took yearly trips back to Beijing to visit their extended family. When Julie left for college, Eva, being the younger sibling, was still in middle school. During this time, the family moved back to Beijing, where Eva completed her schooling. Hence Eva's fluency in Mandarin, and Julie's comparative illiteracy.

The woman they're currently referring to is their mother, who was, by her own metrics, an excellent parent, but by all other accounts, a violently unstable petty tyrant. She is the source of Eva's suicidal ideation and dysmorphia, as well as Julie's overwhelming emotional paralysis.

We won't speak of the father, because, of course, they never did.

EVA. So who are we meeting tomorrow?

JULIE. Amanda, she's like the NGO point-person on this, she's the one that found the document. Wednesday, we train to Yingcheng.

EVA. To meet him.

JULIE. Right.

EVA. And he's the –

JULIE. In the wheelchair, yeah. *(Beat.)* I hate this fucking country.

EVA. No you don't.

JULIE. I do, I hate the fucking… Chinese mentality. It's so goddamn couched, these people, there's no fucking transparency.

EVA. I think you might be – I don't know.

JULIE. What?

EVA. No, I don't know what I'm saying.

THE TRANSLATOR. 'Let's not get into this.'

(Beat.)

JULIE. What do you do for money?

(Beat.)

EVA. Does it matter?

JULIE. No.

EVA. Okay then.

JULIE. Unless it's morally compromised.

EVA. Is there a legal definition for 'morally compromised'? *(Beat.)* Julie, you sort of... don't have the right to that information.

JULIE. Since when?

(Beat.)

EVA. I'm getting room service, you want anything?

JULIE. My sister back?

EVA. Well, she's dead. You're getting a sandwich.

THE TRANSLATOR. Palo Alto, 2006.

JANE. *(Closing the document.)* We're fine.

MARSHALL. *(To* **LARRY.***)* See?

JANE. He was right to bring it to me, Marshall. I'm your chief legal officer.

LARRY. We're fine?

JANE. I mean, it's not ideal. It's decidedly unideal.

LARRY. But this bullet point, 'Zhuangzhi and other hostile actors' – the fact that they showed us, they're talking about targeting dissidents, doesn't that, like, open us up to anything? Like, accusations of... anything?

JANE. By whom?

LARRY. Like, I dunno, the UN?

JANE. You mean the ICC?

THE TRANSLATOR. International Criminal Court.

LARRY. I don't... know?

JANE. The tribunal responsible for prosecuting individuals guilty of war crimes, crimes against humanity and genocide?

LARRY. Yes?

JANE. Have you committed any genocides lately?

LARRY. I don't... think so?

JANE. You're fine.

LARRY. Okay, but –

JANE. Larry, I'm going to let you in on a little secret about international law. The only effectual branch of international arbitration – the only practicable branch – is the one I specialize in. Corporate law. This means that the mechanisms of international arbitration have been built to serve corporate interests. In other words, there are several mechanisms by which *we*, as a multinational, can take someone to trial. There are essentially none that allow anybody to prosecute *us*. So what I'm telling you is: we're fine.

MARSHALL. I could *kiss* you.

JANE. That would be wildly inappropriate and I would sue you.

MARSHALL. Nah you wouldn't.

JANE. No, I'd miss your winning personality.

LARRY. But we're fine?

JANE. *(The PowerPoint document.)* Now, regarding this question of the board –

MARSHALL. No. Nope.

LARRY. We have to, Marsh.

MARSHALL. No, no fucking way. No board.

LARRY. We have to? Right? Jane?

JANE. Gentlemen. Please. *(Beat.)* As your CLO, this is my suggestion. What you'll do is, you'll call a board meeting, and you'll bring the board this document, this PowerPoint.

MARSHALL. But *why* –

JANE. Because, Marshall, you've just told a bunch of Chinese bureaucrats that you'd show the board this document, and it's generally a good idea to keep the promises you've made to Chinese bureaucrats.

MARSHALL. ...that's a fair point, Bollman.

JANE. Thank you. However, as your CLO, I also recommend you bury it in a stack of paperwork. How long's the contract?

LARRY. Around, uh, three hundred pages.

JANE. Perfect. Stick in the Appendix. And this is the most important part. Larry.

LARRY. Yeah?

JANE. After the meeting?

LARRY. Yeah?

JANE. It'd be unfortunate if that document didn't make its way into your records.

LARRY. Huh? Oh. Like – shred 'em?

JANE. As your CLO, I would never tell you to destroy material evidence related to a contract. I'm just saying, if due to a clerical error, that particular appendix were to go astray, well, that would be a shame.

LARRY. Wait, so – am I shredding them?

MARSHALL. Yeah.

JANE. Absolutely not.

LARRY. No?

MARSHALL. No, Larry. You're *not* shredding them.

LARRY. Oh. So –

JANE. Definitely don't shred them.

LARRY. Right. But – what?

MARSHALL. For fuck's – Larry, shred every fucking copy.

THE TRANSLATOR. Beijing, 2012.

EVA. <u>I'll have the chicken with fried noodles, and she'll have –</u>

我要雞肉炒麵，她要 …

Woyao ji rou chao mian, ta yao…

JULIE. *(Pointing to the glass bottle.)* Can we get some bottled water, with a seal, I don't know where you've gotten this from.

EVA. <u>She just wants a plastic bottle with a seal, sorry.</u>

她只想要矿泉水/密封的，麻煩你了。

Tā zhǐ xiǎng yào kuàngquán shuǐ/mìfēng de, máfan nile.

JULIE. I'll have the shrimp fried rice, don't put any MSG in it, and I know you'll say you don't use MSG, but then I leave with a migraine, so can you *actually* not put MSG in it? Thanks.

THE TRANSLATOR. Monosodium glutamate, food enhancer, rumored to cause dehydration and headaches.

EVA. You shouldn't…

THE TRANSLATOR. Studies do not support this.

JULIE. What?

EVA. Forget it.

JULIE. No, what?

EVA. You can't be so blunt with people here.

JULIE. I'm American. We have a global reputation to uphold.

EVA. Well, you look Chinese, people assume you're Chinese.

JULIE. I should fucking hope not. Pass me the hot sauce.

(Beat.)

EVA. Hey, you remember the food matching?

JULIE. Hm?

EVA. You know, the matching thing? With food? You remember this?

JULIE. No.

EVA. Whenever we, like... whenever she served us a plate of something, to be shared between the two of us, she'd insist on absolute equality, so we had to count the grapes, or, or the peas, to make sure we got exactly our share. And she never put odd numbers on the plate.

JULIE. Uh... that didn't happen.

EVA. No, she did this till I was like six.

JULIE. Well, I was there, I was older, that didn't happen. There was a time where you did that, you counted what you ate, but that's 'cause you –

EVA. No, this was earlier, like way earlier.

JULIE. Then you're conflating things.

EVA. No, I –

JULIE. Also can we not – let's not suddenly treat her with *nostalgia*, now she's –

EVA. Jules.

JULIE. – fuck, as though literal decomposition somehow reduces her level of fucking *toxicity* –

EVA. That's not what I –

*(Enter **AMANDA**.)*

AMANDA. I'm late, ugh.

JULIE. No, it's, you're all good. Uh, Eva, Amanda Pearson, International Project Manager for the Digital Freedom Fund. Amanda, Eva Chen, our translator.

AMANDA. What, you guys sisters?

EVA. We, uh, we are, actually.

AMANDA. Oh, for real? You hired your sister?

JULIE. Yep.

THE TRANSLATOR. 'Regretfully.'

AMANDA. That's convenient, your sister's a translator. Nice. Well, nice to meet you, Eva.

EVA. Yeah, ditto.

JULIE. So, any word?

AMANDA. …it's not good. We're down a couple.

JULIE. How many?

AMANDA. Of the fifteen I spoke to, five of them are willing to sign on as does, three willing to be named plaintiffs.

JULIE. Damnit, seriously?

AMANDA. A lot of these people are still under close surveillance, Julie, it's a big ask.

JULIE. Fuck. Well, okay. Fuck, uh. Any of the three willing to travel?

AMANDA. One.

JULIE. The professor?

AMANDA. Yeah, and I gotta say, I think, from what little he's told me, I think his testimony would be pretty compelling.

JULIE. He's willing, I mean he'll testify?

AMANDA. We'll have to negotiate that tomorrow. There's some kind of – he's on board in principle, but there's some kind of reservation.

JULIE. Safety?

AMANDA. He wouldn't say over the phone, I think it's best we discuss it in person.

JULIE. Okay, uh, what about the document? Can we authenticate it?

AMANDA. Well...

JULIE. Amanda! Seriously?

AMANDA. I mean – it's Wikileaks, they have a near-perfect record of document authentication.

JULIE. We can't get up in front of a Dallas jury and say Wikileaks has a – most of these people won't know the diference between Wikileaks and Wikipedia!

AMANDA. That seems like an unfairly harsh judgement on the population of Dallas.

JULIE. You ever been to Texas?

AMANDA. I hiked the Rio Grande.

JULIE. Christ, why are you Australians always so goddamn outdoorsy?

AMANDA. They put something in the water.

EVA. Wait, so, you need to, like, authenticate the document?

JULIE. Eva, I keep telling you, you don't have to –

AMANDA. Jules, it's beyond reasonable doubt that the Head of China Ops saw it.

JULIE. Why don't you let me be the judge on what reasonable doubt entails here? Wikileaks is not beyond reasonable doubt.

EVA. Wait, this thing was presented at a board meeting?

JULIE. Evie.

THE TRANSLATOR. 'Shut up.'

EVA. And there aren't any other copies?

AMANDA. Not with this appendix. For all we know they shredded the rest.

EVA. Oh. Well, it's just, uh – maybe this is stupid, but this thing is dated, there's a date in the header.

JULIE. Eva!

AMANDA. No, Julie – she's –

EVA. Don't – like – don't companies with public stock, don't they have to publish the minutes of board meetings? So, like, couldn't you cross-reference the agenda of the board meeting with the document to prove it's real? And couldn't you check the attendance and prove the guy was there, so he had to have seen it?

(Beat.)

AMANDA. Wow.

JULIE. Huh.

AMANDA. You go to law school?

JULIE. That's, uh.

EVA. No.

JULIE. Shit.

EVA. I majored in Asia Studies.

JULIE. That's good.

AMANDA. Uh, what kinda jobs do you get with that?

EVA. ...this, I guess?

JULIE. Evie.

EVA. Yeah?

JULIE. That's fucking good.

TRANSLATOR. 'I love you.'

EVA. Oh. Okay.

THE TRANSLATOR. Dallas, 2015.

JULIE. Now, everyone in this room agrees that there are human rights abuses going on in China. That's a well-documented fact.

THE TRANSLATOR. There's actually a great deal of debate about the / extent – okay.

JULIE. But the Defense is going to argue that a single bullet point is insufficient evidence of ONYS's criminal collusion. After all, this is the only copy we have access to. How can we prove that Mr. McLaren and his colleagues actually saw this document?

Well, let's look at our exhibits.

Exhibit A, this bullet point, was presented to ONYS board members on July 31st, 2006. Now, because we have access to the public minutes of this board meeting, which is our Exhibit B, you can also see clearly, here, that Marshall McLaren, the head of China Operations, is listed as being in attendance. What does this all mean?

It means Mr McLaren not only saw this document, but he saw it before their contract was renewed. Which means he not only helped to build the Golden Shield, but that he did it in the full knowledge that this was one of the Ministry's central goals. That they specifically and explicitly intended on targeting Zhuangzi activists.

THE TRANSLATOR. Beijing, 2012.

AMANDA. It's sort of ingenious.

EVA. Well, you spend enough time with lawyers –

AMANDA. Dude, you just made our case. Take the compliment.

EVA. Ha, okay, thanks.

(Beat.)

AMANDA. So this was a, uh, surprising WeChat request.

EVA. Well, like, I don't know, it's our only night in Beijing, there's all these bars around, you seemed cool, so, I figured, uh, you'd be the sort of person I'd wanna get trashed and go dancing with.

AMANDA. Can I just clarify something here?

EVA. What?

AMANDA. Like, is this a drink, or like, a *drink*?

EVA. Oh, no, yes, I am definitely trying to fuck you.

AMANDA. Okay, good, I thought so.

EVA. Yeah, there should be no ambiguity about that.

AMANDA. So, okay, I wish people could just –

EVA. Right?

AMANDA. Because it's like, there's enough miscommunication in the world, I don't want to spend all night reading between the lines and like, searching for a sign, or symbol, like, a visual metaphor for whether or not you want to stick your fingers in me, because if you just like say, upfront, what you mean, then like, you don't need to *translate*, you know?

THE TRANSLATOR. I guess I should go.

AMANDA. So I take it Julie's not coming.

EVA. No, she's, uh, she'd be sort of pissed if she knew I was doing this.

AMANDA. Does she not –

EVA. Oh, no, no. That's not – no, she thinks I fuck her colleagues to piss her off.

AMANDA. Do you?

EVA. Uh. Kind of... so, her partner – not like her partner in life, her partner in law, Richard –

AMANDA. Oh yeah, Richard, I know Rich. You and Rich, that's, uh, that's quite a... I mean, not to cast aspersions, he's a lovely guy but, uh, you can do better.

EVA. How much better?

AMANDA. A lot better.

(Beat.)

EVA. Okay, I really wanna ask you like a million questions about your amazing life and your super cool job but first I have to make out with you otherwise I will not be able to concentrate on what you're saying.

AMANDA. Um, that's heartening, but you actually shouldn't.

EVA. Why?

AMANDA. Because you're in a public place and homosexuality was illegal in China until 1997.

EVA. So making out with you would be like a seditious act?

AMANDA. Not anymore. But definitely uncomfortable for the people around you.

EVA. But we can finish these drinks and make out in the bathroom.

AMANDA. We can in fact do that.

EVA. Outstanding. Tell me about your exciting and fabulous job.

AMANDA. My job, uh, my job. It's a lot of advocacy, a lot of... ranting, raving, tweeting. Not a lot of downtime.

EVA. Yeah, I get that vibe.

AMANDA. I work myself to death, it's pretty unsustainable. Blah, enough me, is this, like, your full-time gig? Being your sister's translator?

EVA. Oh. Uh. Well I'm, I just graduated so – I'm between –

THE TRANSLATOR. Should I come back?

EVA. – actually, uh, I'm – I'm a sex worker, I work in the sex industry.

THE TRANSLATOR. Oh.

AMANDA. Oh.

THE TRANSLATOR. Guess not.

EVA. Yeah. I mean, informally? I'm not – uh –

AMANDA. If you don't mind, uh, what exactly...

EVA. I date people.

AMANDA. Oh.

EVA. Uh, specifically, I date these guys, these older guys, rich white guys, and uh, they pay for my rent and my clothes and my food and uh, my everything.

AMANDA. Oh. So you're like a –

EVA. Yeah. Yep.

AMANDA. Do you... do you fuck them?

EVA. Um, I didn't really intend to, when I started out, but then one of them offered me a lot of money, so now, yeah, I do.

AMANDA. All of them?

EVA. One of them I just give blow jobs to, because he's in like his seventies.

AMANDA. Oh.

EVA. Yep. That's uh, what I do for money.

AMANDA. Well, hey, uh, no judgment.

EVA. Oh, feel free to judge me, I'm a terrible person.

AMANDA. I don't really know you at all, but you don't seem like a terrible person.

EVA. I'm sort of like a generally decent person masking like a depraved sociopath.

AMANDA. I feel like this is your way of telling me I shouldn't date you.

EVA. Yeah, it's a, uh, tactic.

AMANDA. I guess it's a good thing you live in D.C.

EVA. Yeah.

AMANDA. And I live in Sydney.

EVA. Yep.

AMANDA. And this is our only night in Beijing.

EVA. Guess so.

AMANDA. Well. *(Downing her drink.)* I feel a sudden and overwhelming urge to powder my nose.

THE TRANSLATOR. 'Meet me in the bathroom.'

Dallas, 2015.

JULIE. Mr. McLaren, I get the sense you're not a fan of ambiguities, so the next question I'm going to ask you is an objective question, a question that deals in facts and figures. How much of your earned revenue this year came from your business in China?

MARSHALL. You'd have to look at the earnings report.

JULIE. I did. It's 46%. You know what else it says in your earnings report? It says that the majority of that money comes from something called 'system infrastructure.' What does that mean, McLaren?

MARSHALL. It means... what it says it means. Infrastructure.

JULIE. So in fact, you weren't just *consulting* with the Ministry. You didn't just sell them an *idea*. When your contract was renewed in 2006, you also sold them a bunch of *stuff*. And all that *stuff*, those millions of routers, and switches, and cables, that's all still in China. And that stuff, that you continue to build, and maintain, and profit from, that stuff is the blood and guts of the Golden Shield. Mr McLaren, you wanna tell us how many shares you own as Head of China Operations?

MARSHALL. I don't know the exact –

JULIE. I can tell you, it's in the insider roster, it's 63,000 shares, that's around 2.8 million dollars. So you also continue to profit from it *personally*.

MARSHALL. Everyone in management / is –

JULIE. That wasn't a question, Mr McLaren, that was a fact. Now, the next question I'm going to ask you is going to be a wholly unambiguous question, a question you can answer with a simple 'yes' or 'no,' do you think you can do that for me?

MARSHALL. I think I can manage that.

JULIE. Did you see this document at the ONYS board meeting on July 31st 2006?

(Beat.)

MARSHALL. I don't remember.

JULIE. You don't remember.

MARSHALL. No.

JULIE. I'll remind you you're under oath.

MARSHALL. Yeah, I'm aware of that.

JULIE. You can remember the dollar value, per share, of your stocks in 2005, but you can't remember seeing this document?

MARSHALL. I mean, come on, we're talking about a bullet point. Can you remember any bullet points you read a decade ago?

JULIE. But you received this document directly from the CCP.

MARSHALL. Not that I recall, not specifically.

(Beat.)

Look, the fact is –

JULIE. Mr McClaren, do you / seriously –

MARSHALL. The fact is that this document, it was one of hundreds – probably thousands – of documents that came across my desk while we were negotiating the contract renewal. I mean, to be honest with you, it was probably thrown in the packet by an intern. God knows if I ever read it.

JULIE. Wouldn't you say that displays corporate negligence on your part?

(Beat.)

MARSHALL. I guess that's for the jury to decide.

JULIE. Actually it's for you to answer.

(Beat.)

MARSHALL. From where I sit, Ms Chen, I made the internet faster for 1.4 billion people. If that's corporate negligence, then I guess I'm negligent.

THE TRANSLATOR. Beijing to Yingcheng, 2012.

JULIE. What'd you get up to last night?

EVA. Nothing. Got trashed.

JULIE. The usual then.

EVA. ...yeah.

> *(Beat.)*

JULIE. I like trains.

EVA. Me too.

JULIE. Calming.

EVA. Mm.

> *(Beat.)*

JULIE. You know, I thought about it. For college. Moving here. With you and mom.

EVA. No you didn't.

JULIE. I did. *(Beat.)* You know, I thought it might be good to... get... culturally reacclimated. So I could have, like, an actual connection to this place. *(Beat.)* Thing is, though, you look at what's going on in this country, it doesn't exactly inspire stirrings of national pride.

EVA. Right.

> *(Beat.)*

JULIE. That was good work by the way, with the thing.

EVA. Oh. Thanks.

JULIE. You ever thought about it? Law school?

EVA. Don't have the grades.

JULIE. Yeah, but I don't know, there's...courses, or, something.

EVA. Just because – forget it.

JULIE. No, what?

EVA. You don't have to give me brownie points for doing a 'smart thing,' Jules. I'm smart. I just don't feel the need to, like, broadcast at it all the time. *(Beat.)* It hasn't been all fun and games, you know. Being the comparatively stupid sibling, you know.

JULIE. ...Eva, you're not – do you honestly think that?

EVA. You're a lawyer, I'm a... whatever.

JULIE. Yeah, but, like, emotional intelligence, you've got me beat. I've got the emotional intelligence of a brick.

EVA. I mean, whatever, that's just transactional logic. You work out what someone wants from you and what you want from them. Then you make the transaction.

JULIE. Christ, dude. Go to law school. Make that logic billable by the hour.

EVA. Yeah. Maybe. *(Beat.)* I'll look into it.

JULIE. You should. *(Laughing.)* Transactional logic. You're pretty messed up, kid, you know that?

EVA. Pot, meet kettle.

JULIE. Ha, yeah. No shit.

(Beat.)

EVA. I mean, like, all things considered. Our childhood. We're pretty well-adjusted.

JULIE. Speak for yourself, man. I'm pretty...

THE TRANSLATOR. Damaged.

EVA. Yeah, well, I'm.

THE TRANSLATOR. Also damaged.

JULIE. But you know, we're… you know.

EVA. Yeah.

THE TRANSLATOR. Not sure on this one. I think it's expressing a kind of… solidarity. Or yearning.

(Beat.)

EVA. So if this guy's testimony, if it's compelling, it could make your case, right?

JULIE. Pretty much.

*(**LI** wheels his wheelchair to the center.)*

EVA. So what do you need him to say?

JULIE. That he's suffering.

End of Act One

ACT TWO

THE TRANSLATOR. I admit I wasn't being totally candid
At the outset
I do have a degree of... professional ego, you see
The hardest part is actually getting it wrong
The moments where you actually hinder communication
Shut down a dialogue
It invalidates your work
Because in those moments, you prove that the very attempt –
Of taking a thought from one place, one culture, one set of given circumstances
And reimagining that thought for another set of circumstances
Well,
You prove that the attempt is futile
That, in reality, there are only false equivalences
You can approximate, but –
That's all it ever is
That's my job, in fact,
Is not really to translate
But to interpret
Not to transmit truth to truth

But to give you informed approximations

Beijing, 2006.

> *(The* **TRANSLATOR** *translates* **LI** *and* **MEI** *dialogue to English.)*

LI. **It has an infrared camera, a spectrograph and a photometer.**

这有一台红外线照相机，一台光谱仪和一台光度计。

Zhè yǒu yìtái hóngwàixiàn zhàoxiàngjī, yìtái guāngpǔyí hé yītái guāngdùjì.

MEI. **Li.**

力。

LI. **This camera is the most important part.**

照相机是最重要的部分。

Zhàoxiàngjī shì zuì zhòngyào de bùfen.

MEI. **Li. Eat something.**

力。吃点东西。

Lì. Chī diǎn dōngxi.

LI. **In ten years, we'll have photographed parts of the universe we've never seen before.**

在未来的十年里，我们会拍摄到宇宙里以前从没有看到过的 部分。

Zài wèilái de shíniánlǐ wǒmen huì pāishèdào yǔzhòulǐ yǐqián cóngméi yǒu kàndàoguò de bùfen.

MEI. **It's not too late for a career change.**

现在改行还不晚。

Xiànzài gǎiháng hái bù wǎn.

LI. **You think I'm smart enough for astrophysics?**

你认为我有资格成为天体物理学家吗？

Nǐ rènwéi wǒ yǒu zīgé chéngwéi tiāntǐ wùlǐ xuéjiā ma?

MEI. **In my opinion, you'd make a terrible astronaut.**

依我看，你会是个很糟糕的宇航员。

Yīwǒkàn, nǐ huì shìgè hěn zāogāo de yǔhángyuán.

LI. Not an astronaut. *(In English, raising his fist like a superhero.)* **An** EXOPLANETEER!

不是宇航员,是EXOPLANETEER!

búshì yǔhángyuán, shì EXOPLANETEER!

MEI. *(Slapping his hand down.)* **Did you forget you have a four year old?**

你忘了你有个四岁的孩子吗?

Nǐ wàng le nǐ yǒu ge sìsuì de háizi ma?

LI. Let her wake and hear! It's not harmful to instil a child with an early love of astronomy.

让她醒来听听,早点让孩子对天文学产生兴趣也挺好的。

Ràng tā xǐng lái tīng tīng, zǎodiǎn ràng háizi duì tiānwénxué chǎnshēng xìngqù yě tǐng hǎo de

(Beat.)

MEI. Did you get the mail?

你拿到信件了吗?

Nǐ ná dào xìnjiàn le ma?

*(**LI** places the stack of mail on the table.)*

What did they do?

他们都做了什么?

Tāmen dōu zuò` le shénme?

LI. We drank tea.

我们只是喝茶。

wo men zhishi hecha.

MEI. What did they ask you?

他们问了你什么?

Tamen wenle ni shenme?

LI. **The questions aren't important. It's just a ritual. They ask a question, I say no, they ask a question, I say no, they give me the mail.**

没什么重要的问题,只是例行公事。他们问一个问题,我说 没有,他们又问另外一个问题,我还说 没有。然后他们就把 信件还给我了。

Méishénme zhòngyào de wèntí, zhǐshì lìxínggōngshì. Tāmen wèn yīgè wèntí, wǒ shuō méiyǒu, tāmen yòu wèn lìngwài yīgè wèntí, wǒ hái shuō méiyǒu. Ránhòu tāmen jiù bǎ xìnjiàn huán gěi wǒle

MEI. **I don't understand.**

我不明白。

Wǒ bù míngbái.

LI. **Mei.**

梅。

Méi.

MEI. **They're not taking Dr Zhang's mail, are they?**

他们怎么不截取张博士的信件?

Tāmen zěnme bù jiéqǔ zhāng bóshì dì xìnjiàn?

LI. **I've explained this to you already.**

我以前给你解释过这些了。

Wǒ yǐqián gěi nǐ jiěshìguò zhèxiē le.

MEI. **So you're the only networks expert in China?**

全国就只有你一个网络专家啊?

Quánguó jiù zhǐyǒu nǐ yīgè wǎngluò zhuānjiā a?

LI. *(Murmured.)* **Your phone.**

你的手机。

Nǐde shǒujī.

MEI. **What?**

怎么了？

Zěnmele?

> (**LI** *puts a finger to his lips, points to her phone.*)

> (*She reluctantly turns it off.*)

LI. **Just in case.**

就怕万一。

Jiù pà wànyī.

MEI. **This is stupid.**

太荒谬了。

Tài huāngmiù le.

LI. **Mei, the government have access to a lot of information.**

梅，政府有办法获取各种信息。

Méi, zhèngfǔ yǒu bànfǎ huòqǔ gè zhǒng xìnxī.

MEI. **Don't talk to me like I'm a child. Everyone knows that. This is 2006, no one bugs phones anymore.**

不要把我当小孩。大家都知道这个。现在都二零零六了，没有人 偷听手机了。

Bùyào bǎ wǒ dāng xiǎohái. Dàjiā dōu zhīdào zhège. Xiànzài dōu èr líng líng liùle, méiyǒu rén tōu tīng shǒujīle.

LI. **I'm trying to explain something to you. Since the announcement about the Olympics, the government**

is cracking down. They're afraid of people 'climbing the wall'.

我想跟你说清楚。自从奥运会宣布以后，政府管得更严了，怕人门翻墙。

Wǒ xiǎng gēn nǐ shuō qīngchu. Zìcóng Àoyùnhuì xuānbù yǐhòu, zhèngfǔ guǎn gèng yán le。Pà rénmén fānqiáng

MEI. What wall?

什么墙?

Shénme qiáng?

LI. The firewall. The government is investing billions of yuan in improving our firewalling system.

防火墙。政府要用数十亿元来加强防火墙系统。

Fánghuǒqiáng. Zhèngfǔ yaoyòng shùshíyì yuán lái jiāqiáng xìtǒng.

MEI. What does this –

这跟 ...

Zhè gēn ...

LI. I teach people to build filtering systems. That's my area of expertise. If you know how to build them, you know how to break through them. That's why our mail is being held.

我教学生建过滤系统。 我是专门搞这行的。如果你知道怎么去建，你肯定就知道怎么去攻破。这就是我们的信被扣留的 原因。

Wǒ jiāo xuésheng jiàn guòlǜ xìtǒng. Wǒshì zhuānmén gǎo zhèhángdeo. Rúguǒ nǐ zhīdào zěnme qù jiàn, nǐ kěndìng jiù zhīdào zěnme qù gōngpdò。Zhè jiù shì wǒmen de xìn bèi kòuliú de yuányīn.

MEI. Li, if you were involved in anything –

力，你要是和这些事有关系 ...

Lì, nǐ yaoshì hé zhèxiē shì yǒuguānxi...

LI. **I am not.**

我没有。

Wǒ méiyǒu.

MEI. **I know. But if you were, you would tell me.**

我明白，但如果有，你一定会告诉我的吧。

Wǒ míngbai, dàn rúguǒ you, nǐ yídìng huì gàosu wǒde ba.

LI. **Of course.**

当然。

Dāngrán.

MEI. **Even if it would put me or Xiao in danger.**

即使这会给小晓或我带来危险。

Jíshǐ zhè huì gěi xiǎo xiǎo huò wǒ dài lái wéixiǎn.

LI. **Then you wouldn't want to know.**

那样的话，你不知道比较好。

Nàyàng dehuà, nǐ bù zhīdào bǐjiào hǎo.

MEI. **It's not up to you. We're a team.**

这不是你一个人的决定。我们是一家人。

Zhè bùshì nǐ yigeren de juédìng. Wǒmen shì yì qi de.

LI. **Of course.**

当然。

Dāngrán.

MEI. **Remember, if you break a promise to me –**

记住，你对我食言的话...

Jìzhù, nǐ duì wǒ shíyán de huà...

LI. I know. I destroy myself.

我知道。我会毁了自己。

Wǒ zhidao. Wǒ hui huǐle zìjǐ.

THE TRANSLATOR. In the first year of their marriage, Li drunkenly kissed a colleague at a staff party. When he broke the news to Mei, she did not cry. Instead, she sat him down and calmly articulated her feelings about breaking a promise to the person you love. Mei explained that when you choose to love a person, you are also making a moral choice about the kind of person you want to be. In loving someone, you destroy your former self and create a new self, in the image of the person you love. As such, every time you break a promise to a person you love, you destroy yourself – at least, the present version of yourself, the self you have created in the image of your lover. Mei said she grew up in a village prone to earthquakes, so she had a high threshold for destruction. Then she kissed him on his eyelids.

LI. Mei. I'm not involved in anything. Once the Olympics are over, things will go back to the way they were.

梅。我没有介入任何事。奥运会结束之后，一切都会恢复原 样。

Méi. Wǒ méiyǒu jièrù rènhé shì. Àoyùnhuì jiéshù zhīhou, yíqiè dou huì huīfù yuányàng.

MEI. The Olympics are in two years. Is it going to be like this for two years?

两年后，奥运会才举行。这两年都要这样吗？

Liǎngnián hòu, Àoyùnhuì cái jǔxíng. Zhè liǎngnián douyao zhèyàng ma?

    (Beat.)

Can I turn my phone on now? I'm losing my game.

我现在可以开手机吗?我的游戏输了。

Wǒ xiànzài kěyǐ kāi shǒujī ma? Wǒ de dānrén zhǐpái shule.

LI. *Ai-ya*. **We can't have that.**

哎呀。那不行。

Āiya. Nà bùxíng.

> *(She turns her phone back on. He watches her.)*

MEI. Why are you staring?

盯着我干什么?

Dingzhe wǒ gàn shénme?

LI. I like watching you play with yourself.

我喜欢看你自己玩自己。

Wo xihuan kan nǐ zìjǐ wán zìjǐ.

MEI. Pervert.

你变态。

Nǐ biàntài.

LI. Give me a kiss.

亲我一下。

Qīn wǒ yīxià.

MEI. Rephrase that.

换句话,说好听点。

Huàn jù huà, shuō hǎotīng diǎn.

LI. Kiss me?

亲我好吗?

Qīn wǒ hǎo ma?

MEI. Almost there.

还不到位。

Hai budaowei.

LI. Please kiss me?

求求你亲亲我吧

Qiú qiú nǐ qīn qīn wǒ ba

> (*They kiss.*)

THE TRANSLATOR. Yingcheng, 2011.

AMANDA. You have a beautiful home.

EVA. She says you have a beautiful home.

他说您的家很漂亮。

Tā shuō nin de jia hěn piàoliang.

LI. Mei has made some recent improvements.

小梅最近布置了一下

Xiǎoméi zuìjìn bùzhìle yīxià

> (**MEI** *nods stiffly.*)

EVA. He says she's redecorated –

MEI. Everything had to be refitted for the wheelchair.

房子不得不改装成适合轮椅的。

Fángzi bùdébù gǎizhuāngchéng shìhé lúnyǐ de.

JULIE. What?

EVA. She said, uh, they had to refit the house, for his wheelchair.

MEI. <u>I'll make some tea.</u>

我去泡茶。

Wǒ qù pào chá.

> (*Exit* **MEI**.)

JULIE. Shall we, uh – Amanda, can you take the lead on this?

AMANDA. Sure. Sure. So, Li, as we discussed, our case will be a lot stronger, uh, the more members of Zhuangzi we can get involved.

EVA. *(Staggered.)* <u>She's saying our case will be a lot stronger, if we can get more members of Zhuangzi involved in the lawsuit.</u>

她说我们的案子会更加强有力，如果我们能让更多庄子成员 参与到诉讼中。

Tā shuō wǒmen de ànzi huì gèngjiā qiáng yǒulì, rúguǒ wǒmen néng ràng gèng duō zhuāng zǐ chéngyuán cānyù dào sùsòng zhōng

AMANDA. We're hopefully looking at a class action, of around, uh, at least ten, fifteen litigants.

EVA. *(Staggered.)* <u>We're hopefully looking at a class action lawsuit involving at least ten litigants.</u>

我們希望有集體訴訟,至少有十個訴訟人參與。

Wǒmen xīwàng yǒu jítǐ sùsòng, zhìshǎo yǒu shígè sùsòngrén bèigào cānyù.

AMANDA. And we're looking at really substantial compensation if we win. You said you've been having financial troubles after your release?

EVA. *(Staggered.)* <u>And you'll get very substantial compensation if we win. You said you've been having financial troubles after your release?</u>

而且您會得到很大的一筆補償，如果我們贏的話。您之前提 過你們有經濟压力？自從你被釋放之後?

Erqie ninhui dedao henda yibi buchang, ruguo women yin dehua. Ni zhiqian tiguo nimen you jingji yali? Zicong nibei shifang zhihou?

LI. <u>My condition – this has all been very expensive. And I can't get a lecturing job anywhere, Mei is our only income now.</u>

我的情况 – 所有的开销都很贵。我也不可能找到教书的工作,梅现在是我们唯一的收入。

Wǒ de qíngkuàng – suǒyǒu de kāixiāo dōu hěn guì. Wǒ yě bù kěnéng zhǎodào jiāoshū de gōngzuò, méi xiànzài shì wǒmen wéiyī de shōurù。

EVA. *(Staggered.)* My condition – this has all been very expensive. And I can't get a lecturing job anywhere, Mei is our only income now.

AMANDA. I'm really sorry to hear that. I want you to know that we're going to do everything we can to make sure you're compensated.

EVA. *(Staggered.)* <u>We will do everything we can to make sure you get compensation.</u>

我们将尽一切努力确保您得到补偿.

Women jiang jin yiqie nuli quebao nindedaobuchang.

LI. <u>Thank you.</u>

谢谢。

xie xie.

AMANDA. That's okay, *bu ke qi*, Uh, so, Julie?

JULIE. Mr Li, the thing we need to ask you about today is about testifying in our court. As you might know, the court system in America is a jury system, which means it'll really strengthen our case to have one of the plaintiffs actually testify, so they can hear firsthand what you've been through.

EVA. <u>The thing we need to ask you about today is about testifying in our court. The court system in America is a jury system, it'll really strengthen our case to</u>

have one of the plaintiffs actually testify, so they can hear firsthand what you've been through.

今天我們要問您關於上庭作證的問題。美國的法庭用的是陪審團系統。让原告作證的話，會讓我們的訴訟更有力。他們可以親耳聽到您的經歷。

Jintian women yao wen nin guanyu shangting zuozheng de wenti. Meiguo de fating yong deshi peishentuan xitong. Rang yuangao zuozheng dehua, huirang women de susong geng youli. Tamen keyi qin'er tingdao ninde jingli.

JULIE. We understand that travelling to America under false pretenses is a pretty big risk for you, but because of your connections in academia we think it might be easier for you than some of the others.

EVA. **We understand that travelling to America under false pretenses is a pretty big risk for you, but because of your connections in academia we think it might be easier for you than some of the others.**

我們理解假借名義去美國対您來說风险很大，但是因為您在學術界的關係，我們覺得您去可能會比其他人更方便。

Women lijie jiajie mingyi qu meiguo duini laishuo fengxian henda, danshi yinwei ninzai xueshujie deguanxi, women juede ninqu keneng hui bi qitaren geng fangbian.

(Beat.)

LI. **I'm willing to travel.**

我愿意去。

Wo yuanyi qu.

EVA. Uh, he's say he's willing.

AMANDA. Oh! Oh, well, uh, that's great. So –

LI. <u>But you cannot interview me here.</u>

但你不能在这里问我问题。

Dan ni buneng zaizheli wenwo wenti.

JULIE. What was that?

EVA. He's saying, uh, you can't do the pre-interview, like, here, in the house.

LI. <u>We can get an office space in Beijing.</u>

我们可以在北京找个地方。

Wǒmen kěyǐ zài běijīng zhǎo gè dìfāng.

EVA. *(To* **JULIE.***)* We can get an office space in Beijing.

JULIE. We're on a tight schedule.

AMANDA. I'm sorry, Beijing is just too risky. I've had meetings monitored there before.

EVA. <u>It's too risky to meet in Beijing.</u>

在北京见面风险太大。

Zài Běijīng jiànmiàn fēngxiǎn taida.

LI. <u>I'm sorry – I am happy to testify and help you fight this company –</u>

对不起 – 我很乐意帮你作证，跟这个公司对抗 –

duibuqi – wohen leyi bangni zuozheng, genzhege gongsi duikang.

EVA. *(Staggered.)* He says he's happy to testify –

LI. <u>– but we have to prepare for this fight somewhere else.</u>

– 但是我们必须在另外一个地方准备。

Danshi women bixu zai lingwai yige difang zhunbei.

EVA. *(Staggered.)* <u>– but we have to prep him somewhere else.</u>

AMANDA. Can you ask if he's concerned about their safety? Because it'll be much safer in his house, in a rural – under controlled conditions, than in a public setting. Particularly if we can get it done in a single day.

EVA. *(Staggered.)* **Are you concerned about your safety? My colleague assures me that it's much safer to conduct interviews here, under controlled conditions, than in a public setting.**

您是擔心你們的安全吗?我的同事很肯定，在這裡问问题会更 安全，比公共場所更好控制。

Nín shì dānxīn nǐmen de ānquán ma? Wǒ de tóngshì hěn kěndìng, zài zhèlǐ wèn wèntí huì gèng ānquán, bǐ gōnggòng chǎngsuǒ gèng hǎo kòngzhì.

LI. **It can't be here.**

在这里不行。

Zài zhèlǐ bùxíng.

EVA. **Why?**

为什么?

Wèishéme?

LI. **I'm sorry, I will do everything you ask, but it can't be here.**

很抱歉，你怎么要求都可以，但就是不能在这里。

Hěn bàoqiàn, nǐ zěnme yāoqiú dōu kěyǐ, dàn jiùshi bùnéng zài zhèlǐ.

JULIE. What's the problem?

EVA. I... I don't know, he's just saying it can't be here, it can't be here, I don't –

(MEI re-enters. She pours tea.)

Thank you.

谢谢。

Xièxiè.

AMANDA. Xiexie.

JULIE. <u>Thank you. It smells wonderful.</u>

谢谢。很香。

Hěn xiāng.

LI. *(To* **EVA.***)* <u>She speaks Mandarin?</u>

她会普通话呀？

Tā huì Pǔtōnghuà ya?

JULIE. Oh, uh, tell him, not really, I don't really speak –

EVA. <u>She speaks a little.</u>

她会说一点。

Tā huì shuō yìdiǎn.

LI. <u>Your accent is very good.</u>

你的口音很标准。

Nǐ de kǒuyīn hěn biāozhǔn.

EVA. He says your accent –

JULIE. Yeah, no, I got that, tell him, uh – **I know**, 我会 búhuì understand some, **Chinese**, 中文zhōngwén, but, I don't, uh – I don't speak well.

LI. <u>Your family's from China?</u>

你老家在中国吗？

Nǐ lǎojiā zài Zhōngguó ma?

EVA. He asked if your family is –

JULIE. Yeah, no, I got that, Evie. <u>My mother.</u>

我的妈妈。

Wǒde māma.

(Beat. Exit **MEI**.*)*

AMANDA. Can you ask him – how much does his wife know about his incarceration?

EVA. <u>How much does your wife know about your incarceration?</u>

關於您坐牢的事，您太太知道多少?

Guānyú nǐ zuòláode shì, Nin taitai zhīdào duōshǎo?

(Beat.)

LI. <u>We've never spoken about it.</u>

我们从来不谈这事。

Wǒmen cónglái bu tán zhè shì.

JULIE. Was that – did he say they've never –

EVA. They've, uh, yes, they've never spoken about it.

JULIE. How – forgive me, Li, how is that possible? You were in detention for – you were gone for five years.

EVA. <u>You were gone for five years.</u>

您五年沒在家。

Nin wǔnián méi zài jiā.

(Beat.)

AMANDA. Where does she think he was for five years?

EVA. <u>Where does she think you were?</u>

她以為你在哪裡?

Tā yǐwéi nǐ zài nǎilǐ?

LI. <u>We've... we've never discussed it.</u>

我们 ... 从没谈过。

Wǒmen... cóng méi tánguò.

EVA. They've just... they've never talked about it.

LI. **I came back... like this.**

我回来 ... 就像这个样子。

Wǒ huílái... jiù xiàng zhège yàngzi.

EVA. He says he, he came back in a wheelchair, so, I guess, they never...

(Beat.)

JULIE. Wait. Wait. Does she even know... does she know he was helping people break through the firewall, that he was denounced? Does she know about Zhuangzi?

EVA. **Does she know about Zhuangzi?**

她知道庄子的事吗?

Tā zhīdao Zhuàngzhì de shì ma?

LI. **I... I don't know.**

我 ... 不知道。

Wǒ...bù zhīdào.

JULIE. Jesus.

LI. **This is the problem.**

关键问题就在这里。

Guānjiàn wèntí jiù zài zhèlǐ.

EVA. So that's why he –

JULIE. Yeah, no, I get it. Jesus, fuck. Fuck, uh, okay, translate this: I understand this is a complicated situation.

EVA. I don't think –

JULIE. Translate the fucking sentence.

EVA. Can I say it, like, in a gentler –

JULIE. No, Evie, because I'm not his shrink, I'm his representation.

EVA. I get that, but if she / doesn't –

JULIE. She already knows, man. They may have some kind of, I don't know, Chinese honor-bound vow of silence around it, but she has a TV in the house, there's no way she doesn't know.

EVA. Okay, but, like, imagine, your husband starts giving testimony about his dissident activity, his *terrorist* activity, in your house –

JULIE. Eva.

EVA. Like –

JULIE. Eva. I am paying you – you are being *paid* – to be my *Translator*. You don't get input on issues I'm having with my client. Now, before he works out how – how much of a *fucking child* you're being, would you kindly translate –

(**MEI** *re-enters with a box of butter cookies.*)

THE TRANSLATOR. For Eva and Julie, the phrase 'fucking child' is particularly loaded. You see, at their mother's funeral two months earlier, Eva, as the child better versed in Chinese culture, was slated to perform the ritual burning. It's a custom in Mahayana funerals for a relative of the deceased to burn a stack of paper money and other object. In this way, it's said, the dead will receive material comforts, in heaven as on earth.

(**MEI** *lays out the cookies.*)

EVA. <u>Thank you.</u>

谢谢。

Xièxiè.

JULIE. <u>Thank you.</u>

谢谢。

Xièxiè.

THE TRANSLATOR. When it came time for the bonfire, Eva approached the pile of paper objects, a can of gasoline and box of matches in hand. She lit a match, but the wind was too high. She lit a second. The same. She lit a third. No luck. The crowd grew restless. As she lit the fourth, Eva suddenly heard her mother's voice, as though she was there beside her, screeching 'that's perfectly good money you're burning!' And there, in the center of the congregation, Eva was seized by an uncontrollable fit of laughter, one which rippled up from a potentially mistakable snort to an all-out cackle, much to the horror of the assembled congregation. Finally, Julie stormed up, muttered 'you're a fucking child,' and set the pile on fire herself.

(Beat.)

*(***MEI** *exits.)*

JULIE. Evie?

EVA. I'm fine, go ahead.

JULIE. Mr Li, you have already endured so much suffering at the hands of this regime.

EVA. *(Staggered.)* **You have already endured so much suffering.**

您已經受了那麼多苦。

Nǐ yǐjīng shòule nàme duō kǔ.

JULIE. I know that this case will take an immense toll on you and your family.

EVA. *(Synchronously.)* **But knowing how much you have suffered –**

雖然您承受了這麼多 ...

Suīrán nǐ chéngshòu le zhème duō...

JULIE. I would not ask you to endure more suffering –

EVA. *(Synchronously.)* **Don't underestimate / how much your wife has endured –**

但不要 / 低估您太太承受的 ...

Dàn búyào dīgū nǐn taitai chéngshòu de...

THE TRANSLATOR. She's mistranslating.

JULIE. – if I was not fully confident –

EVA. *(Synchronously.)* **– your wife must know why you were arrested –**

您太太一定知道您被逮捕的原因 ...

Nin taitai yídìng zhīdào nǐn bèi dàibǔ de yuányīn...

THE TRANSLATOR. – Your wife must know why you were arrested –

JULIE. – that this case will improve the lives of activists around the world –

EVA. *(Synchronously.)* **– which means she will stand by you –**

這意味着，她應該會支持您 ...

Zhè yìwèizhe, tā yinggaihui zhichi nin...

THE TRANSLATOR. *(Synchronously.)* – which means she will stand by you –

JULIE. – by taking a stand against Chinese tyranny –

EVA. *(Synchronously.)* **– no matter the cost.**

不管什麼代價。

Bùguǎn shenme dàijià.

THE TRANSLATOR. *(Synchronously.)* – no matter the cost.

JULIE. – and exposing this regime for what it is.

EVA. *(Staggered.)* <u>**She is clearly a very strong person.**</u>

她明顯是個非常堅強的人。

Tā míngxiǎn shìgè fēicháng jiānqiáng de rén.

THE TRANSLATOR. She is clearly a very strong person.

LI. *(Breaking down.)* <u>**I know. I know.**</u>

我知道，我知道。

Wǒ zhīdào, wo zhīdào.

JULIE. Uh, is that a…

LI. <u>**You're right.**</u>

你说没错。

Nǐ shuō méi cuò

JULIE. Is that a yes?

LI. <u>**I know.**</u>

我知道。

Wo zhi dao.

JULIE. Evie.

AMANDA. Why's he –

JULIE. Is that a yes?

EVA. You can ask your questions here.

THE TRANSLATOR. Dallas, 2015.

JULIE. Mr McLaren and his colleagues knew about the existence of Zhuangzhi. They knew that the Chinese Government explicitly intended to target Zhuangzhi activists through the construction of the Golden Shield. And then they helped build it anyway. Why did they do this? Out of pure and simple greed. Because Mr McLaren and his colleagues valued their bottom line more than they valued the rights and lives of Chinese citizens. Citizens like the next person you'll be hearing from. My client, Mr Dao Li.

THE TRANSLATOR. Dallas, 2015.

RICHARD. When was your first contact with the Ministry of Public Security?

EVA. *(Staggered.)* **When was your first contact with the Ministry of Public Security?**

您第一次和公安部接触是什麽時候?

Nin dìyīciì heé gōng'ān bù jiēchù shì shenme shíhòu?

LI. **I can't remember exactly.**

记不清楚了。

Ji buqingchu le.

EVA. *(Staggered.)* I can't remember exactly.

RICHARD. Then, roughly, what year was it?

EVA. **Around what year?**

是哪一年?

shi nayi nian?

LI. **Computer science in Beijing is a small field. I've had many connections in the ministry. Even some former students.**

北京的计算机行业很小，我在安全部部有很多认识的人。

其中有很多还是我以前的学生。

Běijīng de jìsuànjī hángyè hěn xiǎo, wǒ zài ānquán bù bù yǒu hěnduō rènshì de rén. Qízhōng yǒu hěnduō háishì wǒ yǐqián de xuéshēng.

EVA. *(Staggered.)* Computer science in Beijing is a small field. I've had many connections in the ministry. Even some former students.

JULIE. Okay, uh, so, don't say that.

EVA. *(Staggered.)* **Don't say that.**

不要提這個。

Buyao ti zhege.

LI. **You said I should tell the truth.**

你说要我说实话。

Nishuo yaowo shuo shihua.

EVA. *(Staggered.)* You said I should tell the truth.

JULIE. That particular truth isn't relevant, and it could cause problems.

EVA. **It isn't relevant, and it could cause problems.**

這一點不重要，還有可能帶來不必要的麻煩。

Zheyidian bu zhongyao, haiyou keneng, dailai bubiyao de mafan.

LI. **If it's not relevant, how can it cause problems?**

如果不重要，为什么会带来麻烦？

Ruguo buzhongyao, weishenme hui dailai mafan?

EVA. *(Staggered.)* If it's not relevant, how can it cause problems?

RICHARD. That kinda thing can be used against us, that he has connections in government, the defense can spin it.

EVA. There's not really a word / for –

LI. **Isn't it worse if I withhold information?**

隐瞒不是更不好吗？

Yinman bushi geng buhao ma?

EVA. *(Staggered.)* Isn't it worse if I withhold information?

RICHARD. You absolutely shouldn't withhold anything.

EVA. *(Staggered.)* <u>**You absolutely shouldn't withhold anything.**</u>

確實不應該隱瞞。

Queshi buyinggai yinman

JULIE. Just don't volunteer information. Simply answer the question.

EVA. **Just don't volunteer information. Simply answer the question.**

但是也不用主動告訴他們。回答問題就可以了。

Danshi ye buyong zhudong gaosu tamen. Huida wenti jiu keyile.

LI. <u>**How do you want me to answer this question?**</u>

你想要我怎么回答这个问题?

Nǐ xiǎng yào wǒ zěnme huídá zhège wèntí?

EVA. *(Staggered.)* How do you want me to answer this question?

JULIE. It's not about how I *want* you to – just, tell us the first time it was a formal meeting, the first time it was, you know, targeted.

EVA. **The first time it was a formal meeting, the first time it was, you know, targeted.**

跟我們講第一次正式會面的時候。第一次您被, 嗯, 針對的 時候。

Gen women jiang diyici zhengshi huimian de shihou. Diyici nin bei, en, zhendui deshihou.

LI. <u>**What do you mean, targeted?**</u>

针对是什么意思?

Zhendui shi shenme yisi?

EVA. What do you mean, targeted?

RICHARD. The first time they interrogated you.

EVA. <u>The first time they interrogated you.</u>

他們第一次審問您的時候。

Tamen diyici shenwen ninde shihou.

LI. <u>No one interrogated me.</u>

没人审问过我。

Meiren shenwen guo wo.

EVA. He says, uh, no one interrogated him.

RICHARD. What?

LI. <u>I was called in for questioning but it was never an interrogation exactly.</u> (*Laughing.*) <u>We drank tea.</u>

他们问了我一些问题，但那不能算是审问。（笑）我们只是 喝茶。

Tamen wenle wo yixie wenti, dan nabuneng suanshi shenwen. Women zhishi hecha.

EVA. (*Simultaneously.*) I was called in for questioning a few times but it wasn't an interrogation. We drank tea.

RICHARD. They drank tea. Of course. They drank tea.

THE TRANSLATOR. Palo Alto, 2013.

JANE. When I say call me back, you / have to –

MARSHALL. I'm busy, Bollman.

JANE. You have to call me back.

MARSHALL. I'm busy, someone's suing us?

JANE. Yes, I've been trying / to –

MARSHALL. Who's suing us?

JANE. Eight Chinese dissidents.

MARSHALL. What?

JANE. Eight –

MARSHALL. I heard you – fucking, what?

JANE. Eight Chinese dissidents are suing us for criminal collusion with the Chinese government.

MARSHALL. The – how? What? In China?

JANE. In Texas.

MARSHALL. ...*how?*

JANE. It has to do with... pirates. *(Beat.)* It's something of a legal loophole.

MARSHALL. We pay you to foresee loopholes – did you just say *pirates*?

JANE. Yes, well, there's stranger precedent in the history of American legislation. For instance, it's technically still illegal for a donkey to sleep in a bathtub.

MARSHALL. What the fuck does that have to –

JANE. Absolutely nothing. I'm just a font of legal trivia.

MARSHALL. What have they got on us?

JANE. *(Handing.)* This floated up on Wikileaks.

MARSHALL. But, but, we shredded these. We shredded these. Didn't we shred these?

JANE. I am certainly surprised by their reappearance.

MARSHALL. We did! We fucking shredded them!

JANE. Did you leave a copy lying around?

MARSHALL. No!

JANE. Did someone on the board leave a copy lying around?

MARSHALL. Bollman, I saw it with my own eyes, after the meeting, we gathered them and we fucking shredded them. Are we going to trial?

JANE. Hopefully, it won't come to that.

MARSHALL. Yeah? What's fucking hopeful about it?

JANE. We're going to propose a settlement – a generous settlement – and pray the matter doesn't make it any further.

MARSHALL. So we're gonna pay them to shut up.

JANE. Yes, well, we lawyers prefer the term 'settle.'

THE TRANSLATOR. D.C., 2013

JANE. So. Brass tacks. As you know, I represent an organization with the net worth of a Scandinavian nation's GDP, and as such, we have absolutely no interest in engaging with this trivial, though admittedly imaginative, bit of litigation. By the by, my compliments, very wily.

JULIE. *(To* **RICH**.*)* You didn't tell me she was this patronizing.

RICHARD. She's British.

JULIE. Still.

JANE. I'm happy to report that our organization is willing to offer your merry band of Chinese terrorists an exceedingly generous settlement, in exchange for, well, blah blah, keep it out of the press, you get the gist.

RICHARD. How generous?

>   (**JANE** *writes a number on a piece of paper.*)
>
>   (**RICH** *takes it.*)
>
>   (*He looks at it.*)
>
>   (*He passes it to* **JULIE**.*)*
>
>   (*Beat.*)

(**JULIE** *slides it back.*)

JULIE. We're not settling.

THE TRANSLATOR. 'I'm not settling.'

RICHARD. Jules.

JULIE. We're not settling.

RICHARD. Would you give us a second?

JULIE. We don't need a second. Jane, I appreciate you coming all this way. There's the door.

JANE. I think you'd be wise to listen your colleague, Ms Chen.

JULIE. And I think you're fucking scared. *(Beat.)* CLO for a multinational, former top-shelf barrister, and you've never seen anything like it. You don't know how to try this. You don't know how to *begin* trying this.

JANE. Ms Chen, respectfully, *you've* never seen anything like this. You're in torts.

JULIE. That's right. We are. And we're gonna try this like we would any other civil suit. Duty, breach, harm, causation. Damages.

JANE. We'll bury you in paperwork.

JULIE. Bring it. We're gonna try this thing, Bollman, and we're gonna *win*. We're gonna drag your organization's name through the mud, we're gonna *expose* your collusion, we're gonna royally piss off the Chinese government, and more importantly, we're gonna *win*. And when we do – we're coming to you for twice this figure.

(**JANE** *gets up to leave.*)

JANE. As a self-professed expert in torts, you might wanna look up the definition of a class action. It typically involves multiple plaintiffs. Plaintiffs with names. Not 'Does One through Eight.'

JULIE. Oh, we'll have named plaintiffs, don't you worry about that. Plaintiffs and testimony.

JANE. *(Laughing.)* You're not telling me you're gonna get a dissident out of China to testify in a civil court in Dallas? *(Beat.)* Are you? *(Beat.)* You're getting someone out of China?

JULIE. We'll be in touch. There's the door.

*(Beat. **JANE** goes to leave.)*

JANE. *(To **RICHARD**.)* This is a crusade. It's senseless, and it's at the expense of your clients. Prevail upon your colleague to see some sense.

JULIE. He doesn't control me.

RICHARD. *(Shrugging.)* It's true. I'm the looks of the operation.

JULIE. Hey, Bollman. How do you sleep at night?

JANE. ... I'm sorry?

JULIE. I said how do you sleep at night?

(Beat.)

JANE. *(Coolly.)* I have one of those tempur-pedic mattresses.

*(**JANE** leaves.)*

JULIE. What? What's that face?

RICHARD. That's my 'you just turned down ten million dollars' face.

JULIE. We'll get twenty. *(Beat.)* And it's not about the money.

RICHARD. You do know that money is one of the binding principals of a lawsuit. A plaintiff is wronged, they are therefore awarded financial damages. And sometimes, from those damages, we the lawyers actually get paid our legal fees.

JULIE. Landmark case, Rich. We're trying international human rights law as torts. It's not about the money.

RICHARD. Yeah, yeah, it's about doing the right fucking thing, goddamn it. *(Beat.)* You sure Dao feels that way?

JULIE. What's that supposed to mean?

RICHARD. I mean that your client is a guy in a wheelchair who can't get a lecturing job with a stack of medical bills and a young daughter.

JULIE. He's not in this for the money, Rich. He was – he's an activist. He's fighting for the rights of his people.

RICHARD. Is that something he actually said, or something you've inferred?

(Beat.)

JULIE. Hey, Rich. That's pretty good.

RICHARD. What?

JULIE. Stack of medical bills. I can use that.

THE TRANSLATOR. Dallas, 2015.

JULIE. I want to talk for a moment about what compensation could do for Mr Li. You can see that the injuries Dao sustained in prison have left him permanently confined to a wheelchair. This has obviously had an enormous personal cost. It also has a very literal cost. There's a stack of medical bills. There's disability insurance. And because of his time in prison, Mr Li struggles to get teaching work. He struggles to make the money he needs to raise his young daughter. All of this, simply because he was helping others to exercise their universal right to free speech, a right that you and I take for granted in this country.

THE TRANSLATOR. Yingcheng, 2015.

> *(The TRANSLATOR translates LI and MEI dialogue into English.)*

LI. I ... I may spend some time in America soon. For a conference.

我 ... 我过一阵子要去美国呆一段时间。参加一个会。

Wǒ...wo yěxǔ bùjiǔ jiù qù Měiguó dāi yíduàn shíjiān.

Qu cānjiā yígè hui.

MEI. What kind of conference? *(Beat.)* With your American colleagues?

什么会? *(Beat.)* 跟你的美国同事?

Shénme yàng de huì? *(Beat.)* Gēn nǐ dì měiguó tóngshì?

LI. Yes.

嗯。

Shi。

MEI. Which university are they from?

他们是哪个大学的?

Tāmen shì nǎge dàxué de?

LI. Caltech, in California.

加州理工, 在加利福尼亚。

Jiāzhōu lǐgōng, zài jiālìfúníyǎ.

> *(Beat.)*

MEI. They're not professors. Who are they?

不是教授。他们是谁?

Tāmen búshì jiàoshòu. Tāmen shì shéi?

LI. It's late.

时间不早了。

Hěn wǎnle.

MEI. Are they other terrorists?

他们也是恐怖分子吗?

Tāmen yěshì kǒngbùfènzi ma?

LI. I'm not a terrorist.

我不是恐怖分子。

Wǒ búshì kǒngbùfènzi.

MEI. Then what are you? What did you do?

那你是什么? 你干了什么?

Nani shi shenme? Ni zuo le shenme?

LI. I thought you knew.

我以为你都知道了.

Wǒ yǐwéi nǐ yǐjīng zhīdàole

MEI. I knew you were lying to me. But I chose to believe you. I thought that whatever you were doing, it couldn't be that dangerous. Because I never thought you would be so selfish, that you would value your ideals more than the safety our family.

我当时就知道你在骗我。但我选择相信你。我以为不管你在 做什么，都不会那么危险，可我从没想过你会如此自私，你会为了理想不顾家人的安危。

Wǒ dāngshí jiù zhīdào nǐ zài piàn wǒ. Dàn wǒ xuǎnzé xiāngxìn nì. Wǒ yǐwéi bùguǎn nǐ zài zuò shénme, dōu bù huì nàme wéixiǎn, kě wǒ cóng méi xiǎngguò nǐ huì rúcǐ zìsī, nǐ huì wèile lǐxiǎng bùgù jiārén de ānwéi.

LI. I wasn't being selfish. I was helping people. I was teaching people.

我并不是自私。我在帮大家,我在教育大家。

Wǒ bìng bùshì zìsī. Wǒ zài bāng dàjiā, wǒ zài jiàoyù dàjiā.

MEI. Who were you helping? Anonymous people on the internet? Are they more important than your family?

你帮了谁？在网上无名无姓的人？他们比你的家人更重要 吗？

Nǐ bāngle shéi? Zài wǎngshàng wúmíng wú xìng de rén? Tāmen bǐ nǐ de jiārén gèng zhòngyào ma?

LI. It doesn't matter who they are! I'm a teacher! Sharing my knowledge is my duty! How can I remain silent when I understand what the government is doing?

他们是谁并不重要！我是个教授！分享我的知识是我的责 任！当我明白政府在做什么时，我怎么能保持沉默？

Tāmen shì shéi bìng bù chóng yào! Wǒ shìgè jiàoshòu! Fēnxiǎng wǒ de zhīshì shì wǒ de zérèn! Dāng wǒ míngbái zhèngfǔ zài zuò shénme shí, wǒ zěnme néng bǎochí chénmò?

MEI. And what about your duty to your family?

那你对你家人的责任呢？

Nà nǐ duì nǐ jiārén de zérèn ne?

LI. China is also my family! *(Beat.)* I never meant to put you in danger. I was just teaching people how to break through the firewall. Everybody is doing it. I didn't think they'd arrest me.

中国也是我的家人！*(Beat.)* 我从来没有故意把你带入危险之中. 我只是教人们如何突破防火墙。人人都这样做。我没想到他 们会把我抓起来。

Zhōngguó yěshì wǒ de jiārén! *(Beat.)* wǒ cónglái méiyǒu gùyì bǎ nǐ dài rù wéixiǎn zhī zhōng. Wǒ zhǐshì jiào rénmen rúhé túpò fánghuǒqiáng. Rén rén dōu zhèyàng zuò. Wǒ méi xiǎngdào tāmen huì bǎ wǒ zhuā qǐlái.

MEI. **But now you're putting us in danger again. I heard them asking you questions. They want you to testify in court.**

但现在你又把我们陷入危险。我听到他们问你问题。他们希 望你在法庭上作证

Dàn xiànzài nǐ yòu bǎ wǒmen xiànrù wéixiǎn. Wǒ tīng dào tāmen wèn nǐ wèntí. Tāmen xīwàng nǐ zài fǎtíng shàng zuòzhèng.

LI. **Xiao Mei, if we win this case, we'll have enough money to leave China. You won't have to work anymore. We could go anywhere – England, Europe. Xiao Xiao can get a good college degree. We can start again.**

小梅, 如果我们赢了这个案子，我们会得到足够的钱离开中 国。你不必再工作了。我们可以去任何地方 – 美国，欧洲。小晓可以去上一个好的大学。我们可以重新开始。

Xiǎoméi, rúguǒ wǒmen yíngle zhège ànzi, wǒmen huì dédào zúgòu de qián líkāi zhōngguó. Nǐ bùbì zài gōngzuòle. Wǒmen kěyǐ qù rènhé dìfāng – měiguó, ōuzhōu. Xiǎo xiǎo kěyǐ qù shàng yīgè hǎo de dàxué. Wǒmen kěyǐ chóngxīn kāishǐ.

MEI. **So now you want to leave China? You're a hypocrite. Where's your patriotism now?**

你现在想离开中国了？你是个伪君子。你的爱国主义现在在 哪里？

Nǐ xiànzài xiǎng líkāi zhōngguóle? Nǐ shìgè wèijūnzǐ. Nǐ de àiguó zhǔyì xiànzài zài nǎlǐ?

LI. **They've beaten it out of me.**

被他们毒打没了。

Bèi tāmen dúdǎ méile.

(Beat.)

MEI. **Did they do this to you in prison? Why won't you tell me?**

这是他们在监狱里干的吗？你为什么不告诉我

Zhè shì tāmen zài jiānyù lǐ gàn de ma? Nǐ wèishéme bù gàosù wǒ?

LI. **If we leave China, we can start again. I made a mistake. I am working hard to fix it.**

如果我们离开中国，我们可以重新开始。我犯了一个错误。我正在努力弥补。

Rúguǒ wǒmen líkāi zhōngguó, wǒmen kěyǐ chóngxīn kāishǐ. Wǒ fànle yīgè cuòwù. Wǒ zhèngzài nǔlì míbǔ.

(Beat.)

MEI. <u>**I waited for you for five years. I'm tired of waiting. Go to America.**</u>

我等你等了五年。我不想再等了。你去美国吧。

Wǒ děng nǐ děngle wǔ nián. Wǒ bùxiǎng zài děngle. Nǐ qù měiguó ba.

(Beat.)

LI. **We've been working on this case for three years. They need me.**

我们这个案子已经忙了三年。他们需要我。

Wǒmen zhège ànzi yǐjīng gōngmangle sān nián. Tāmen xūyào wǒ.

MEI. *I* **need you.**

我需要你。

Wǒ xūyào nǐ.

> (Beat.)

LI. (*As he's leaving, almost to himself.*) **I can't survive without you.**

没有你我活不下去的。

Méiyǒu nǐ wǒ huóbuxiàqù de.

> (**MEI** *cries.*)

> (*She leaves.*)

THE TRANSLATOR. Dallas, 2015.

JULIE. I have one final thing to say to you about my client, and it's a… a tragic, recent development. As a result of his participation in these proceedings, Dao and his wife Mei have recently separated, which is an incredible burden, given his condition. Ladies and gentlemen, I'll remind you what you heard in Mr McLaren's testimony – ONYS makes around $50 billion a year. Think about what a fraction of that money could do for my client.

> (*Fracturing locations:*)

RICHARD. (*To* **LI.**) So once you're in the witness box, they'll ask you to raise your right hand.

EVA. **Once you're in the witness box, they'll ask you to raise your right hand.**

一旦你进入见证箱，他们会请你举起右手。

Yīdàn nǐ jìnrù jiànzhèng xiāng, tāmen huì qǐng nǐ jǔ qǐ yòushǒu.

RICHARD. And then they'll ask you: Do you Swear to Tell the Whole Truth and Nothing But the Truth, So Help you God? And you'll answer:

EVA. <u>**And then they'll ask you: Do you Swear to Tell the Whole Truth and Nothing But the Truth, So Help you God? And you'll answer:**</u>

然后他们会问你：你向上帝发誓，你所说的全部都是事实 吗？然后你说

Ránhòu tāmen huì wèn nǐ: nǐ xiàng shàngdì fāshì, nǐ suǒ shuō de quánbù dōu shì shìshí ma? Ránhòu nǐ shuō:

> (**LI** *says nothing.*)

RICHARD. Mr Li?

EVA. Professor Li?

李老师？

LI. (*Tersely.*) <u>**I understand. Can we move on?**</u>

我明白. 可以了吗？

Wǒ míngbái. Ke yi le ma?.

EVA. I understand. /Can we move on?

MARSHALL. I don't understand why I have to stick around for this.

JANE. You're the defendant.

MARSHALL. I have shit to do, you know, I can't just be sitting around in a Dallas courtroom, waiting for the fucking cripple / to tell his sob story.

JANE. Oh, Christ, McLaren.

MARSHALL. Waste of my fucking time. I mean what the hell are they trying to get out of this anyway, huh? Money. We tried to give them money.

JANE. They want to make a statement.

MARSHALL. Yeah, well, some kinda fucking statement, when they fucking lose this thing. (*Beat.*) Jane, there's no chance of them winning, right? Cuz you said to me, to my face, that there's no chance in hell of them winning.

JANE. There's... a very small chance.

MARSHALL. Very *small*? Since when did no chance become very *small*?

JANE. To be frank, McLaren, you didn't... come off terribly well on the stand.

MARSHALL. The hell is that supposed to mean? I did exactly what we prepped for, I evaded all her fucking questions, I said I had no memory of the fucking thing, which you and I both know –

JANE. – is a totally plausible claim and I'd rather you not tell me otherwise because then I'd know that you'd just knowingly perjured yourself in a court of law –

MARSHALL. So what the hell is that supposed to mean, that I didn't come off terribly well?

JANE. It just means that you're not terribly... how should I put this... likable.

> (*Beat.*)

MARSHALL. Yeah, no shit, I'm not likable. No shit. (*Beat.*) Is that gonna be a problem?

JANE. Well. Probably not.

MARSHALL. Jane. You gotta tell me. Is it a problem?

RICHARD. Then we'll move on to your arrest and time in prison.

EVA. <u>Then we'll ask about your arrest and time in prison.</u>

然后我们会问你关于你被逮捕和监禁的时间。

Ránhòu wǒmen huì wèn nǐ guānyú nǐ bèi dàibǔ hé jiānjìn de shíjiān.

RICHARD. Jules?

JULIE. *(To* **LI**.*)* Right, so, Mr Li. How long were you held in detention?

EVA. <u>How long were you held in detention?</u>

你被拘留了多久?

Nǐ bèi jūliú le duōjiǔ?

LI. <u>From 2006 to 2011, for fifty three months.</u>

从二零零六年到二零一一年,总共五十三个月。

Cóng èr líng líng liu nián dào èr líng yī yī nián, zǒnggòng wǔshísāngè yuè.

EVA. From 2006 to 2011, for fifty three months.

JULIE. And during that time, you lost your ability to walk?

EVA. <u>And during that time, you lost your ability to walk?</u>

在这期间,你是否失去了行走的能力?

Zài zhè qíjiān, nǐ shìfǒu shīqùle xíngzǒu de nénglì

LI. <u>Yes.</u>

是。

Shi.

EVA. Yes.

JULIE. How did that happen?

EVA. <u>What happened?</u>

怎么发生的?

Zěnme fāshēng de?

LI. <u>There were a number of contributing factors.</u>

有各种影响因素。

Yǒu gèzhǒng yǐngxiǎng yīnsù.

EVA. There were a number of contributing factors.

(*Beat.*)

JULIE. Tell him he has to actually describe the incident.

EVA. <u>You have to describe the incident.</u>

你必须描述这事件

Nǐ bìxū miáoshù zhè shìjiàn

LI. <u>I was abused.</u>

我被虐待了。

Wǒ bèi nüèdàile.

EVA. I was abused.

JULIE. …in what way?

EVA. <u>In what way?</u>

怎么样的虐待?

Ze me yang de neudai?

LI. <u>You said that if I don't want to talk about it, I don't have to.</u>

Nǐ shuōguò rúguǒ wǒ bùxiǎng tíqǐ zhèxiē, wǒ méi bìyào

EVA. You said that if I don't want to talk about it, I don't have to.

JULIE. You… don't.

RICHARD. No, that's why we're asking you these questions again now, so you can tell us if there's anything you're not comfortable answering.

EVA. <u>That's why we're asking you these questions again now, so you can tell us if there's anything you're not comfortable answering.</u>

这就是为什么我们现在再次问您这些问题，这样您可以告诉 我们有什么您不想回答的 。

Zhè jiùshì wèishéme wǒmen xiànzài zàicì wèn nǐ zhèxiē wèntí, zhèyàng nín kěyǐ gàosù wǒmen yǒu shé me nín bùxiǎng huídá de

JULIE. But just saying you were physically abused is a bit… vague, the jury won't understand what you mean.

EVA. Jules.

JULIE. He has to go into more detail. *(To* **EVA.***)* Evie. Tell him that.

EVA. <u>She says you have to go into more detail. Or the jury will be confused.</u>

她说你必须详细形容, 否则陪审团会搞不清楚。

Tā shuō nǐ bìxū xiángxì xíngróng, fǒuzé péishěn tuán huì gǎo bù qīngchǔ.

LI. <u>What do you want? I'm here. I'm saying what you want me to say. Is there nothing that I'm allowed to keep private?</u>

你还想要什么? 我在这。我在说你要我说的话。我没有任何 隐私了吗?

Nǐ hái xiǎng yào shénme? Wǒ zài zhè. Wǒ zài shuō nǐ yào wǒ shuō dehuà. Wǒ méiyǒu rènhé yǐsīliǎo ma?

EVA. What do you want from me? I'm here. I'm saying what you want me to say. Is there nothing that I'm allowed to keep private?

JULIE. Why he is getting so upset?

LI. <u>Why did you talk about my wife?</u>

你为什么提起我的妻子?

Nǐ wèishéme tíqǐ wǒ de qīzi?

RICHARD. What was that?

EVA. *(To* **JULIE.***)* He wants to know, uh, why you brought his wife up, in your opening remarks.

JULIE. To give the – I had to give the full picture, your wife is part of the context of this case, what we need to make clear is, is that compensation is warranted –

EVA. *(Staggered.)* **She wanted to give the jury context.**

她是为了幫陪審團了解背景。

Tā shì wèile bāng péishěntuán liǎojiě Bèijǐng.

LI. **I told you I didn't want my family involved! I shared that information with you in *private*, in *confidence*!**

我说过不要牵扯到我的家人！我是私下跟你说的，保密的！

Woshuoguo buyao qianche dao wode jiaren! Woshi sixia genni shuode, baomide!

EVA. *(Staggered.)* I told you I didn't want my family involved! I shared that information with you in *private, in confidence*!.

LI. **Is this why you tried to persuade me that my wife would stand by me, no matter the cost?**

这就是你试图说服我的原因？你说我的妻子會支持我，不管 什麼代價？

Zhè jiùshì wèishéme nǐ shìtú shuōfú wǒ, wǒ de qīzi yīnggāi huì zhīchí wǒ, bùguǎn shénme dàijià?

THE TRANSLATOR. *(Staggered.)* Is this why you tried to persuade me that my wife would stand by me, no matter the cost?

EVA. **No that wasn't –**

那不是 –

Na bu shi –

LI. **You thought if she left me you could use it as additional evidence?**

你以为如果她离开我你可以用它作为额外的证据吗？

Nǐ yǐwéi rúguǒ tā líkāi wǒ nǐ kěyǐ yòng tā zuòwéi éwài de zhèngjù ma?

THE TRANSLATOR. *(Staggered.)* You thought if she left me you could use it as additional evidence?

LI. <u>Is this a game to you? You know what I'm risking to be here? You know what I've sacrificed?</u>

你觉得这是游戏吗？你知道我在这里冒的风险吗？我牺牲了什么吗？

Nǐ juédé zhè shì yóuxì ma? Nǐ zhīdào wǒ zài zhèlǐ mào de fēngxiǎn ma? wǒ xīshēngle shénme ma?

THE TRANSLATOR. *(Staggered.)* Is this just a game to you? This is my life. You know what I'm risking to be here? You know what I've sacrificed?

RICHARD. Could you –

JULIE. Will someone PLEASE FUCKING TRANSLATE?

THE TRANSLATOR. Gee, I'm trying.

EVA. <u>It wasn't her. It was me. I said that.</u>

不是她。是我。我说过的。

Bùshì tā. Shì wǒ. Wǒ shuōguò de.

THE TRANSLATOR. *(Staggered.)* It wasn't her. It was me. I said that.

EVA. <u>It wasn't her. She didn't know. I mistranslated. I wanted you to say yes. I was wrong. I'm sorry.</u>

不是她。她不知道。我误译了。我想让你说是的。我错了。对不起。

Bùshì tā. Tā bù zhīdào. Wǒ wù yìle. Wǒ xiǎng ràng nǐ shuō shì de. Wǒ cuòle. Duìbùqǐ.

THE TRANSLATOR. *(Staggered.)* It wasn't her. She didn't know. I mistranslated. I wanted you to say yes. I was wrong. I'm sorry.

JULIE. What are you saying to him? Evie, what are / you –

EVA. *(Breaking down.)* I mistranslated.

JULIE. What? When?

EVA. I mistranslated.

JANE. Look. They don't have a leg to stand on legally. It's a flimsy argument and they know it. But if Dao comes off well, and you don't, there is always the possibility that – and it's slim, but there is a possibility – that the jury will sympathize with him and not you. And, well, ignore the facts.

   (Beat.)

MARSHALL. That's a possibility, then.

JANE. As I've said, their argument is thin, and I think, as an American, they're more likely to sympathize with you than with a Chinese plaintiff. But... as a human being...

   (Beat.)

MARSHALL. You offered them ten?

JANE. Yes.

MARSHALL. Offer them twenty. I gotta get back to fucking work.

JULIE. The fuck were you thinking, Evie?

EVA. It was –

JULIE. You realize you could have jeopardized our entire fucking case? What the fuck were you thinking?

EVA. I just – I knew you really needed his testimony, and I just thought it'd be, like, more efficient –

JULIE. More *efficient*?? You thought that mistranslating what I was saying to my fucking client, you thought emotionally manipulating him would be more *efficient*?

EVA. I mean, it was, wasn't it? I'm the one who got him here!

JULIE. By *lying* to him!

EVA. I didn't *lie*, I just said she probably already knew about his denouncement, so she'd stand by him no matter what, I mean, you're the one who brought her up in your opening remarks when he said he didn't want his family involved, now you're like badgering him about his time in prison, which he clearly doesn't wanna / talk about –

JULIE. For the last fucking time, Eva, you are not a fucking lawyer. I need him to talk about the abuse, it's how we demonstrate grievous harm. See, that's a *legal strategy*. You telling my client that his wife would never leave him, that's a naïve and frankly fucking *idiotic* statement, one that could now fuck up my case, to say nothing of my client's *life*.

(Beat.)

EVA. Is he is still gonna testify?

JULIE. I don't know, fuck, I don't know. *(Beat.)* Where the fuck am I gonna get a Mandarin translator in Dallas?

THE TRANSLATOR. You called?

EVA. Julie, I – I can still do it.

THE TRANSLATOR. I'm always available.

JULIE. Are you fucking crazy, Evie? I can't put you up on the stand with him now, you have completely destroyed your credibility.

EVA. No, no, I can still help you with this, Jules, if you just let me talk to him –

JULIE. No.

EVA. I can fix it, if you'd just –

JULIE. You can't *fix* it by *talking*. Sometimes things get *broken*, and no amount of *talking* is gonna magically *fix* it. *(Beat.)* Now, I have a justifiably pissed-off client to manage and a translator to find, so would you please just get the fuck out of here.

(Beat.)

EVA. Well, that's just – that's... fine. *(Beat.)* I mean, I'm just sorry I can't continue helping you wage, like, your whole war against, against *Chinese tyranny*.

(Beat.)

JULIE. ... I don't like your tone, there, Evie.

EVA. What tone is that, Jules?

JULIE. What –

EVA. What might I be insinuating there, with my *tone*?

JULIE. ... Jesus, Evie. Really?

EVA. Well, like, I don't know, I'm asking you, what might I be insinuating?

JULIE. Oh, right. Because, right. Because I chose a career, in, in *international litigation*, yeah, that's about right, as an *elaborate revenge plot*, is that the fucking *implication*?

EVA. Oh, no, because it's like just a total coincidence that two months after –

JULIE. Jesus –

EVA. – *two months after* we put her in the fucking ground –

JULIE. Jesus, Eva.

EVA. – and you call me up to be your *Translator*, I mean, what was the idea here, you give me this *bailout*, and we, we take on our *Chinese oppressor*, sisters, hand in hand –

JULIE. You are a fucking child.

EVA. No, no, I *was*. I was a *fucking child*, and you *left*, you *left* me with that *woman*.

JULIE. What the fuck was I supposed to do?

EVA. *Get me out of there.*

JULIE. And do what? Raise a 10-year-old? As a freshman? Does that sound like a reasonable fucking solution to you, Eva?

EVA. You... you've could've done *something*.

JULIE. Like *what*?

EVA. Like, like *visited* once in a while – that was the time for a fucking *bailout*, Jules – you could've done *something*, you could've – I *needed you* and you *left* me, you left me alone in a foreign country with a fucking monster, and it's worse what you did, because she was just ignorant, okay, she was an ignorant tyrant, but you fucking *knew*, you *knew* what she was like, and you left me anyway. And I'm really messed up now, Jules, she messed me up good, and it's too late, there's too much history, I'm all fucked up and you can't fix me.

(Beat.)

JULIE. Well, Evie, you know, now that you've alerted me to the sheer *magnitude* of my crimes against you, systematically fucking all of my colleagues does seem like a mature response. *(Beat.)* What do you do for money?

EVA. I can't...

JULIE. Why?

EVA. Because you won't –

JULIE. I won't? I won't what? I won't be *proud* of you?

*(**EVA** exits.)*

JULIE. Is that it, Evie? I won't be *proud?* I won't be fucking *proud?*

(A long beat. **JANE** *enters.)*

JANE. Bad time?

JULIE. Couldn't be better.

(Beat.)

JANE. I've been authorized to offer you a revised figure.

JULIE. We reject it.

JANE. It's twenty.

(Beat.)

JULIE. He was really something on the stand, your guy. 'I don't remember, maybe an intern did it.'

JANE. It's reasonable doubt.

JULIE. Yeah, but, you gotta admit, the jury's gonna *loathe* that guy. I couldn't have *dreamt* of a better villain.

JANE. You didn't pin him. Not beyond reasonable doubt.

JULIE. Then why the revised figure?

JANE. I'm trying to help you.

JULIE. Ha. *(Beat.)* We reject your offer.

JANE. Julie. Come on. You're on a crusade at the expense of your clients and you know it, all they want is / compensation for –

JULIE. Don't tell me what's in my client's best interests.

JANE. – what they've endured, what kind of humanitarian are you? *(Beat.)* You once asked me how I sleep at night.

JULIE. Yeah.

JANE. I sleep at night in the knowledge that small deeds are better than sweeping gestures. I sleep at night because I get these behemoths to play by the rules. And that's *hard*, Julie. That's harder than whatever it is you people do. 'Fighting the good fight.'

(*Beat.*)

JULIE. We're rejecting your offer.

JANE. Well. Worth a shot. (*Beat.*) If you ever decide to join us soulless corporate sharks, Chen, do let me know. Honestly, I think you'd be better suited to it. It has a kind of moral clarity that humanitarianism precludes.

(**JANE** *exits. A weird shift.*)

THE TRANSLATOR. Hi.

JULIE. Fucking – !

THE TRANSLATOR. Sorry.

JULIE. Christ. You scared the shit out of me. (*Beat.*) Oh, you're the –

THE TRANSLATOR. That's me.

(*Beat.*)

JULIE. Did you... just get here?

THE TRANSLATOR. That's a funny question.

JULIE. It is?

THE TRANSLATOR. You're aware, I assume, that your conception of time has certain linguistic aspects.

JULIE. Uh. Does it?

THE TRANSLATOR. Yes, well, English relies largely on tenses to situate things in time – did you *just* get here, for instance. Mandarin, on the other hand relies largely on context. A shared understanding of where events fall in time. So to translate from Mandarin to English, you also have to translate from objective time to, well, grammatical time. You have to build your own structure. I just think that's... funny.

(*Beat.*)

JULIE. You're a pretty weird guy, huh.

THE TRANSLATOR. (*Laughing.*) I guess I am.

(*Beat.*)

JULIE. Listen, uh, I don't have time to get anyone else, my translator quit like two hours ago, so I'm kind of scrambling here. Just, be as one-to-one as possible, okay? Don't embellish.

THE TRANSLATOR. Of course.

JULIE. And I don't really have time to give you the context, so. You don't have to understand the case, is what I'm saying.

THE TRANSLATOR. Sure.

JULIE. But, uh, you don't happen to have any strong feelings about the Chinese Communist Party, do you?

THE TRANSLATOR. I don't have any strong feelings.

JULIE. Oh. Good.

(*Beat.*)

THE TRANSLATOR. <u>Do you swear to tell the whole truth, in the name of God?</u>

你向上帝发誓，你所说的全部都是事实吗？

Nǐ xiàng shàngdì fāshì, nǐ suǒ shuō de quánbù dōu shì shìshí ma?

LI. <u>Yes.</u>

是。

(Beat.)

*(**JULIE** walks up.)*

THE TRANSLATOR. What happened to the other translator?

(Beat.)

JULIE. Family emergency.

THE TRANSLATOR. That's a real shame.

JULIE. Yeah. It is.

*(To **LI**.)* Mr Li. How long were you held in detention?

THE TRANSLATOR. <u>How long were you held in detention?</u>

你被拘留了多久?

Nǐ bèi jūliú le duōjiǔ?

LI. <u>From 2006 to 2011, for fifty three months.</u>

从二零零六年到二零一一年,总共五十三个月。

Cóng èr líng líng liu nián dào èr líng yī yī nián, zǒnggòng wǔshísāngè yuè.

THE TRANSLATOR. From 2006 to 2011, for fifty three months.

JULIE. And during that time, you lost your ability to walk?

THE TRANSLATOR. <u>And during that time, you lost your ability to walk?</u>

在这期间,你是不是失去了行走的能力?

Zài zhè qījiān, nǐ shìbushì shīqùle xíngzǒu de nénglì?

LI. <u>Yes.</u>

是。

Shi.

THE TRANSLATOR. Yes.

JULIE. How did that happen?

THE TRANSLATOR. What happened?

发生了什么?

Fāshēng le shénme?

LI. There were a number of contributing factors. The muscle strength in my legs deteriorated significantly while I was in prison.

有各种影响因素。我在监狱的时候，腿的肌力有所衰退。

Yǒu gèzhǒng yǐngxiǎng yīnsù. Wǒ zài jiānyù de shíhòu, tuǐ de jīlì yǒusuǒ shuatuì.

THE TRANSLATOR. There were a number of contributing factors. The muscle strength in my legs deteriorated signifcantly while I was in prison.

JULIE. Was there a particular incident that exacerbated this deterioration?

THE TRANSLATOR. Was there a particular incident that exacerbated this deterioration?

有没有发生什么加重减退的事情?

Dàodǐ yǒu méiyǒu fāshēng shénme jiāzhòng jiǎntuì de shìqíng?

LI. Yes.

有。

You

JULIE. What was the incident?

THE TRANSLATOR. What was the incident?

什么事情?

Shénme shìqíng?

LI. <u>**I was forced to stand in the prison yard for thirty hours.**</u>

我被迫在监狱院子里站了三十个小时。

Wǒ bèipò zài jiānyù yuànzilǐ zhànle sānshígè xiǎoshí.

THE TRANSLATOR. *(Staggered.)* I was forced to stand in the prison yard for thirty hours.

JULIE. Until your legs collapsed?

THE TRANSLATOR. <u>**Until your legs collapsed?**</u>

直到你的腿虚脱了?

Zhídào nǐde tuǐ xūtuōle?

LI. Yes.

JULIE. Did the prison guards know your legs had weakened before they made you do this?

THE TRANSLATOR. <u>**Did the prison guards know your legs had weakened?**</u>

监狱的看守知道你的腿已经衰退了吗?

Jiānyù de kānshǒu zhīdao nǐde tuǐ yǐjīng shuaitui le ma?

LI. <u>**Yes, I had asked to see a doctor.**</u>

知道。我之前要求看医生。

Zhīdào. Wǒ zhiqian yāoqiú kànyisheng.

THE TRANSLATOR. Yes, I asked to see a doctor.

JULIE. And instead of letting you see a doctor, they made you stand in the yard?

THE TRANSLATOR. <u>**And instead of letting you see a doctor, they made you stand in the yard?**</u>

但他们没让你看医生,反而让你罚站。

Dan tamen mei rang ni kanyisheng, fan er rangni fazhan?

LI. Yes.

JULIE. Thank you. No further... sorry. I'm not finished. (*Beat.*) Mr Li, while you were imprisoned, did you endure other forms of physical abuse?

THE TRANSLATOR. <u>While you were imprisoned, did you endure other forms of physical abuse?</u>

你坐牢的时候有没有受到其它形式的身体虐待？

Nǐ zuòláo de shíhòu yǒu méiyǒu shòudào qítā xíngshì de shēntǐ nüèdài?

(*A long beat.*)

JULIE. Ask him again.

THE TRANSLATOR. <u>While you were imprisoned, did you endure other forms of physical abuse?</u>

你坐牢的时候有没有受到其它形式的身体虐待？

Nǐ zuòláo de shíhòu yǒu méiyǒu shòudào qítā xíngshì de shēntǐ nüèdài?

LI. Yes.

JULIE. Beatings?

THE TRANSLATOR. (*Staggered.*) <u>Beatings?</u>

挨打吗？

Āidǎ ma?

LI. Yes.

JULIE. Forced feeding?

THE TRANSLATOR. (*Staggered.*) <u>Forced feeding?</u>

强迫进食？

Qiǎngpò jìnshí?

LI. Yes.

JULIE. Electric shocks?

THE TRANSLATOR. *(Shorter stagger.)* **Electric shocks?**

电击?

Diànjí?

LI. Yes.

JULIE. Starvation?

THE TRANSLATOR. *(Shorter stagger.)* **Starvation?**

挨饿?

Āi è?

LI. Yes.

JULIE. Sleep deprivation?

THE TRANSLATOR. *(Shorter stagger.)* **Sleep deprivation?**

剥夺睡眠?

Bōduó shuìmián?

LI. Yes.

JULIE. Solitary confinement?

THE TRANSLATOR. *(Synchronously.)* **Solitary confinement?**

单独监禁?

Dāndú jiānjìn?

LI. Yes.

JULIE. Sexual assault?

THE TRANSLATOR. *(Synchronously.)* **Sexual assault?**

性侵犯?

Xìngqīnfàn?

LI. <u>I was not raped.</u>

我没被强奸。

Wǒ méi bèi qiángjiān.

THE TRANSLATOR. (*Staggered.*) I was not raped.

LI. <u>I was never raped.</u>

我从没被强奸。

Wǒ cóng méi bèi qiángjiān.

THE TRANSLATOR. (*Staggered.*) I was never raped.

JULIE. But you were assaulted?

THE TRANSLATOR. <u>But you were assaulted?</u>

但你被侵犯过?

Dàn nǐ bèi qīnfànguò?

LI. <u>There was an incident where, where four guards, they stripped me of my clothes.</u>

有一回,有四个看守,他们撕破了我的衣服。

Yǒuyìhuí, you sìgè kānshǒu, tāmen sīpòle wǒ de yīfú.

THE TRANSLATOR. (*Staggered.*) There was an incident where, where four guards, they stripped me of my clothes.

LI. <u>The guards... they played with my genitals... and...</u>

看守们 … 玩弄了我的生殖器 … 还有 …

Kānshǒumen… wánnòng le wǒ de shēngzhíqì…háiyǒu…

THE TRANSLATOR. (*Staggered.*) The guards…they played with my genitals… and…

LI. <u>They pulled at my pubic hairs, and…</u>

他们扯了我的阴毛。还有 …

Tāmen chěle wǒ de yīnmáo, and…

THE TRANSLATOR. *(Staggered.)* They pulled at my pubic hairs.

LI. **And then, one of the guards, he took my toilet brush, and... and he...**

然后其中的一个看守，他拿了我的马桶刷，来，他来，

Ránhòu qízhōng de yígè kānshǒu, tā nále wǒ de mǎtǒngshuā, lái, tā lái...

THE TRANSLATOR. And then, one of the guards, he took my toilet brush, and...and he...

LI. **This isn't right. I can't continue – this isn't right.**

这不对。我不能再说下去了...这不对。

zhebudui. Wǒ búnéng zài shuōxiàqùle...zhebudui.

THE TRANSLATOR. He's saying he can't continue, this isn't right, you promised.

JULIE. No further ques – can we take a brief recess?

LI. **This isn't right.**

这不对。

Zhebudui.

JULIE. Can we have a brief recess?

THE TRANSLATOR. *(To the Audience.)* This isn't right.

LI. **This isn't right.**

这不对。

Zhebudui.

JULIE. **Mr Li, I'm sorry.** We're finished. We're finished.

道先生，对不起。

Dāo xiānsheng, duìbùqǐ.

End of Act Two

ACT THREE

THE TRANSLATOR. 三个和尚没水喝
(Sān gè héshàng méi shuǐ hē.)
The image it's supposed to paint
Three monks
Or, three holy men, I don't assume to –
Three holy men are carrying a bucket of water
Together
Up the side of a mountain
But because they're all trying to carry it,
To equally bear the weight of it
They spill it
All of it
And so... they have no water to drink
The English equivalent, I suppose, is something like
'Too many cooks spoil the...'
Right
But
You can see it's not really the same thing
It's not the same thing at all

JULIE. The decision you make here today is going to set a very important precedent.

Not just here in Texas, but around the world. So I appeal now to your human decency. I want you to think about what Li has suffered. And I want you to imagine what you'd hope a jury would decide, were you in his shoes.

The world is watching you.

(To **RICHARD.***)* We'll need to file a notice of Appeal.

RICHARD. Jules.

JULIE. I think it's worth getting some heavy-hitters, some folks who are big in the federal circuit, 'cause you know ONYS will be doing the same.

RICHARD. Jules, come on.

JULIE. I know what you're gonna say about the cost, but if we can drum up some more press, get the right legal team together, I think we can take this thing all the way to the / Supreme court –

RICHARD. Jules, Jules – will you just stop? We're not going to Appeals.

JULIE. What?

RICHARD. He's on a flight back to China. Jules, it's over. We lost. You understand? We lost.

(Beat.)

JULIE. Then we'll get someone else.

RICHARD. Jesus, Jules.

JULIE. What, you think there aren't more people in China affected by this, people won't wanna speak out? Because everyone in China is affected by this, Rich. Every single Chinese citizen. You know the kinda shit they're doing now? AI censors, banning Wikipedia, a fucking social credit system? It's getting worse not better, okay, we can't just stop fighting this just because one Dallas jury –

RICHARD. Jesus, Jules, are you even listening to yourself? You couldn't *get* anyone, remember? Dao was your guy, okay? And you fucked it up!

JULIE. My sister fucked it up!

RICHARD. *Eva* didn't hound our client until he broke down on the stand, Eva sure as hell didn't turn down a twenty-million dollar settlement! *(Beat.)* Jane told me.

JULIE. You went to Bollman behind / my back?

RICHARD. For God's – it's not *behind your back*, I'm your co-counsel, and *you* went behind *my* back when you opted not to disclose the fact that defense had offered us a revised figure at the eleventh hour, the figure we were purportedly aiming for, the figure we should have fucking accepted!

JULIE. How many times do I have to tell you it's not about the fucking money!

RICHARD. Then what the hell is it about, Jules? Tell me what it's about!

JULIE. It's about letting them know someone's watching! It's about letting them know they can't just get away with it! It's about showing them that the Internet isn't just some, some *autonomous entity* –

THE TRANSLATOR. *(To the Audience.)* I don't claim to interpret.

JULIE. – it's not just this nebulous amoral *thing*, hovering around in the ether –

THE TRANSLATOR. *(To the Audience.)* Is that helpful?

JULIE. – the internet is *people*! It's *people* building *things*! And those *people* are causing other people immense fucking *suffering*!

THE TRANSLATOR. *(To the Audience.)* Am I helping you?

RICHARD. Who are we showing, Jules? The jury? The Chinese? Who? ONYS? You think this'll make 'em think twice about, what, their, their corporate governance? You know what might have accomplished that, Jules? Making 'em pay twenty million dollars for their sins! That might've accomplished *something*! *(Beat.)* You know the worst part of all this, Jules? I don't think you have the faintest idea *what* you're doing it for. Me, at least I'm honest about why I'm in this game, I'm in it for the money. But you? I don't think you give a damn about China, or the CCP, or ONYS. I don't think you could give two shits about the Golden Shield. And I think Evie, I think she's way off the mark on this one, I don't think this is some kind of warped revenge plot, no, deep down, Julie, this is just about wanting to win. And you'll step on anyone to get there.

JULIE. She told you about our – she barely knows you.

RICHARD. Actually, she knows me quite well. *(Beat.)* Eva's known me *quite* well for... for about four years.

(A long beat.)

EVA. *(On the phone.)* Heyyy, so you wouldn't happen to be in D.C. and down for a fuck, would you?

AMANDA. Uh, ha, no, I'm in Sydney, where it is a wildly inappropriate time for a booty call.

EVA. Right. Sorry.

AMANDA. But thank you for the charming offer.

EVA. Any time.

AMANDA. Are you okay?

EVA. Not really, no.

AMANDA. I'm sorry. Is it the trial?

EVA. I'm not at the trial. And I'm drunk.

AMANDA. Okay. Did something happen?

RICHARD. Oh, and while you're being morally affronted about – about a business arrangement between two consenting / adults –

JULIE. That's my fucking *sister*, Rich.

RICHARD. – would you ask yourself if it's any more exploitative than what you just did to Li up there on that stand? *(Beat.)* The thing is, what I'll do for money, what Eva will do for money: that has its limits. What you'll do in the name of righteousness… I just don't know anymore, Julie. I honestly don't.

EVA. So I just had this, like, epiphany, and I was, like, oh my god, I have to tell Amanda, she'll totally love this, so, like, I had this epiphany that the reason why I'm good at translating – the reason I'm supposed to be good at translating, anyway – is the same reason I'm good at fucking people for money. Because in both cases, right, people are, like, paying me, essentially, to not have my own thoughts. I'm just this like this empty fucking… conduit. For other people's… bullshit. And where I get into trouble, where the problems start, is when I forget that I'm just a conduit and start thinking that I'm like an actual human being, with a brain. And actually the world would be much better off if I was just like – like if I was just a mouth and a cunt. And I thought – you know who'd like that? Amanda. *(Beat.)* You'd like that wouldn't you? If I was just this like disembodied mouth and cunt.

AMANDA. No.

EVA. Really? Cuz I'd be pretty, like, portable. Long-distance wouldn't be a problem. You could put me in your hand luggage.

AMANDA. Well. I miss you too. *(Beat.)* Evie, what's going on?

EVA. So you wouldn't like if I was just like a mouth and cunt?

AMANDA. Look, as you know, I'm a big fan of both your mouth and your cunt. But I am also a big fan of you as a thinking human being. *(Beat.)* I don't want you to be a conduit, Evie.

THE TRANSLATOR. Oh.

AMANDA. I mean in an ideal world, you'd just be you, and I'd be me, and we'd be... us... and conduits can get fucked.

THE TRANSLATOR. Oh.

AMANDA. And I am fully aware of the irony of saying that down a phone line. *(Beat.)* Evie? You still there?

EVA. *(Crying.)* That's a really fucking nice thing to say.

AMANDA. Occupational hazard, I'm afraid. Activist. Nice by trade.

LARRY. Cheers.

MARSHALL. *Mazel tov.*

EVA. So... How 'bout it?

AMANDA. How about... what? *(Beat, laughing.)* Phone sex?

EVA. Or, I dunno. Something more... involved.

AMANDA. You wanna incorporate toys?

EVA. No, like. Fuck, I'm bad at this.

(Beat.)

AMANDA. Oh. I mean, we live on different... continents.

EVA. Yeah, but, come on. It's the digital age.

AMANDA. I just hadn't even considered that. With you. Because of, like, what you do.

EVA. Oh.

AMANDA. Yeah.

EVA. Is it a problem for you?

AMANDA. I mean, in like a hypothetical realm, no, but in a, um, in a personal realm, I think, yeah, it might be a problem.

LARRY. Poor bastard.

MARSHALL. Can't get into that line of thinking. Onward and upwards.

LARRY. Hey, no, I'm appreciative of the outcome here, just, you know, he's uh, he's a poor bastard.

MARSHALL. We're all poor bastards. It's a question of scale.

EVA. Forget it.

AMANDA. No, hey –

EVA. I'm gonna hang up now.

AMANDA. Don't.

EVA. It's not, uh – I –

AMANDA. Can we just – fuck, let's just back up, okay? Let's talk about it.

EVA. ...like, as in?

AMANDA. As in, you say why you do it. I'll say why I have a problem with it. And then, like, we'll see. *(Beat.)* How about I go first? / I'm afraid your job means I can only think of a relationship as a series of transactions.

THE TRANSLATOR. I'm afraid your job means you can only think of a relationship as a series of transactions.

(Beat.)

EVA. Oh. *(Beat.)* I'm doing it because it's how I make money. Which is necessary. Money is necessary. *(Beat.)* / I'm doing it because it's easier than failing at something else.

THE TRANSLATOR. I'm doing it because it's easier than failing at something else.

AMANDA. Okay. *(Beat.)* See, that wasn't so hard.

MARSHALL. Four hundred percent.

EVA. That was the hardest thing I've ever done.

MARSHALL. We made the internet four hundred percent faster for 1.4 billion people. Where's the conversation about that? Huh? Where's our fucking accolades for that?

LARRY. You don't have to / convince –

MARSHALL. If you went up to any guy on the street, any guy, out in Guangzhou or fucking Shanghai, you said to them, hey, mister, we can either make your wifi four times faster or reduce online censorship, you know which one they'd pick? Maybe some knuckles get bruised, maybe a terrorist loses his legs, but four times faster, for you and your eight fucking kids and their eight fucking kids, you know which one they'd pick?

LARRY. Marsh. We won.

MARSHALL. I'm just saying. Efficiency is good. *Efficiency* is a public fucking good. I don't appreciate being treated like a fucking villain for improving the lives of a billion fucking people, just because people are too fucking *stupid* to understand what it is we *do*. Censorship will always exist in China. All *we* did is we made it four times faster. *(Beat.)* You think I'm a villain, Larry?

LARRY. Nah, man.

MARSHALL. You can tell me if you do. I don't give a shit. Maybe I am a fucking villain. I don't know.

(Beat.)

LARRY. Marsh, look. Would we do it the same way, doing it over? Maybe, maybe not. But a decade on, we're a net good in China, you know? I mean, Google, Yahoo, they couldn't cut it in China, but we could. And we're a net good. And that's something to proud of, you know? That's a reason to celebrate.

MARSHALL. You've changed your fucking tune.

LARRY. Have I?

MARSHALL. I mean time was, you were reining me in, voicing your moral fucking scruples.

LARRY. Yeah, well. That was 2006. I mean, you were right, Marsh. I couldn't see at the time but... this is the way it's heading.

MARSHALL. What way is that?

LARRY. Decentralization. I mean, that's the future, right? Blockchain, universal wifi, it's all headed that way. And it's not gonna mean decentralization of power. Power's always gonna be centralized. But it won't be the Chinese government. It won't be any government. It's gonna be us. We'll have the power, Marsh. So we just gotta use it for good. And for the most part, Marsh, I think we really do. For the most part, I think... I think, all things considered, within reason... I think we're doing a good job.

(Beat.)

MARSHALL. You're smarter than you let on, you know that, Larry?

LARRY. I'm just drunk, man.

(Beat.)

MARSHALL. I've been a dick to you.

LARRY. Nah, man.

MARSHALL. This isn't an apology. It's just an acknowledgement, okay? It's what makes me good at what I do, but it doesn't change the fact that I ... I'm a dick.

LARRY. Hey. *(Raising his glass.)* Water under the bridge.

MARSHALL. / Water under the bridge.

THE TRANSLATOR. 事过境迁

SHI GUO JING QIAN.

(Beat.)

LARRY. And seeing as it's, like, water under the bridge and all, uh, would this be the appropriate moment to tell you that, uh, when I, uh, photocopied the contract for the board meeting, I may or may not have, it was so long ago, who really knows, but I may have, uh, left the, uh, original in the photocopier? *(Beat.)* Would this be a good moment to tell you that?

(Beat.)

EVA. How's the new practice?

JULIE. It's shit. Soulless corporate shit. *(Beat.)* Honestly, it's a relief. *(Beat.)* How's tricks? *(Beat.)* Sorry, I shouldn't –

EVA. It's what I do, so. Tricks are… fine.

(Beat.)

JULIE. You know you / could always –

EVA. Jules, why'd you call? What is this?

(Beat.)

JULIE. So, if you were still thinking about law school –

EVA. I'm not.

JULIE. …okay, anyway, one of the first legal concepts you get taught is intractability. Intractable disputes. Like, that sometimes a dispute's just so convoluted, or the implications are so far-reaching, it's just totally beyond arbitration. And the best thing you can do is just… quit. But I've always been like, fuck intractability, you know? Because nothing should be too big, too messy, too ugly, for the *law*. That's what the law's for. The law's supposed to say, like, here's this convolution, and here's how we deal with it. And I guess what I'm trying to say here is, I think… I think family is the same. Like even when it feels broken, there has to be a *way*. You know? Because that's just… that's what family is. Family can't be *intractable*.

EVA. Oh.

JULIE. So couldn't we – I don't know – could we find a way? To be family? *(Beat.)* Because we went through it *together*. Like we have this ocean of shit, decades of shit, and no-one will ever understand, and even if we tried to explain it, it wouldn't mean what it does, to *us*, you know? Because it's you and me, Evie. It's our history.

> *(Beat.)*

EVA. Yeah, I'm just… I'm just not sure that having, like, shared trauma with someone is a particularly good reason to keep having a relationship. *(Beat.)* You don't even like me.

JULIE. Of course I do.

EVA. Okay, well, honestly, Jules, I don't like you.

> *(Beat.)*

JULIE. We don't have to *like* each other. Families don't *like* each other. They, you know.

> *(Beat.)*

THE TRANSLATOR. *(Out.)* Love is an interesting construct, linguistically. Lots of languages have multiple words for love: Romantic. Familial. Carnal. Interestingly enough, in both Mandarin and English, there's only really one word. And it's pretty much all-encompassing. 爱 (ai.) is both past and future. Love is a circle and a line.

> *(Enter **MEI**, with a bag.)*

> *(She dusts a table.)*

*(Enter **LI**.)*

*(**MEI** looks up.)*

That's, uh, something like, 'well'.

*(**MEI** scratches her ear.)*

That's 'I couldn't stand living with my brother's wife.'

*(**LI** gives the slightest nod, and turns away.)*

That's 'I've been destroyed.'

*(**MEI** puts her bag down.)*

That's 'I'll stay.'

*(**MEI** places a hand on his shoulder.)*

Uh... I think that's a, uh, a blanket expression of care.

*(**MEI** helps **LI** into the sofa.)*

This one I don't think I can... it's somewhere between 'I need you' and 'there is no recovering from this'.

*(**LI** kisses **MEI** on the forehead.)*

THE TRANSLATOR. That one...

*(**MEI** kisses **LI** on the forehead.)*

Not sure. Maybe 'I'm afraid.'

*(**MEI** kisses **LI** on his eyelids.)*

No, that's not...

*(**LI** kisses **MEI**'s face.)*

Hm.

*(**LI** kisses **MEI**'s eyelids.)*

I'm not really sure.

EVA. Is this what you actually want, Jules? Like, do you actually want a relationship with me? Or is this just about doing right thing? *(Beat.)* Because you don't always have to do the right thing, you know.

JULIE. Yeah, I do.

EVA. Why?

JULIE. Because what kind of world would that be? If people just gave up on doing the right thing because it's *hard*? Because it *hurts*?

EVA. I'm not talking about the world. I'm talking about us.

(Beat.)

JULIE. So, what? We just quit? At being family?

EVA. I don't know. Maybe.

(Beat.)

JULIE. But I feel like... we're... tangled up.

EVA. Yeah.

JULIE. So that might be... harder.

EVA. Yeah.

JULIE. And maybe if we just... developed a system, or boundaries, for communicating, then... that would... help.

(Beat.)

EVA. I don't think so.

(Beat.)

JULIE. Oh.

*(**EVA** picks up her coat.)*

EVA. I guess...

THE TRANSLATOR. Talk to her.

JULIE. Yeah.

THE TRANSLATOR. Talk to her.

*(**EVA** leaves.)*

End of Play

www.ingramcontent.com/pod-product-compliance
Lightning Source LLC
Chambersburg PA
CBHW072009290426
44109CB00018B/2186